The Science of Spiritual Healing

From personal development

to global development

Daniel Perret

It is not recommended that this book and its exercises be
used by people with mental health problems.

© 2010 Daniel Perret
Edition : Books on Demand GmbH
12/14 rond-point des Champs Elysées
75008 Paris, France
Imprimé par Books on Demand GmbH
Norderstedt, Allemagne

ISBN 978-2-8106-11805
Dépôt légal : december 2010

This book has also been published by BOD
in German and French.

God is a feeling

Grace brings healing

and

Love is showing us the way.

With my eternal gratitude to Robert S. 'Bob' Moore and to
Ignatius de Loyola.
My thanks to Anni Moore, Eva Høffding and Helen Rytz for
feedback after reading the manuscript &
to Claude Diolosa for many discussions on the subject.
My special thanks to Marie Perret for sharing this journey & for
correcting and editing this English version.

I would like to thank Jaap Koning for his permission to use the
idea of the cover design – similar to the one he designed for
my book on sound healing.

Daniel Perret – The Science of Spiritual Healing

Every aspect of our development is linked to other people, not only to an introverted self. We have something that can bring us together in order to spread healing to the entire earth.

When we look at the development of any person, this cannot be an isolated development. That development must be linked to other people, and to the universe.

Bob Moore

Spiritual Healing is an intuitive science based on facts and precision.
I feel that this science, which is probably as old as human kind, is somehow always at its beginning.
It is a 'living' science, constantly renewing itself in order to remain an experience, a felt knowledge, as Bob used to say.

Daniel Perret – The Science of Spiritual Healing

Table of Content

Introduction

From personal to global development

On an atomic level as on the level of our aura we are only energy. Energy does not ever have any boundaries. We share it with all of creation: the very same energy is everywhere. We do not own that energy; it connects us with everything, with every living being. Whatever we do for ourselves affects every other part of creation.

The word 'spiritual' comes from 'spirit' and is equivalent to 'universal intelligence' or 'the divine'. We must realise that the word 'spiritual' is not the property of this or that religion, it is a universal heritage.

My approach aims to be that of an integrated science, that combines western scientific methods and discoveries (including those of Quantum Physics) and the science of observing consciousness that we have in Tibetan Buddhism. In writing a book on the science of Spiritual Healing I am attempting to go beyond the schemes and criteria of western science, especially when it ignores the findings of Quantum Physics. When we research into the field of Spiritual Healing we combine the approach of western science (third person research) with the experience of the observer himself (research at the level of the first person).

I will concentrate on this. It would be beyond the scope of this book to include a vast amount of quotations from other authors or a bibliography of ten pages. I have done this in my previous book 'Roots of Musicality'. Many interesting books have been written on the subject of energy medicine that other authors have presented. I cannot include everything here. My sources are essentially of an oral nature and have seldom been written down. My major source is (Bob) Robert S. Moore's teachings that I followed for twenty years, between 1979 and 1999 and in some way still do. My other sources, largely stemming from Bob's approach, are my own experiences as a researcher, therapist and teacher. I can therefore largely base my conclusions on my experience of working with my students whom I have been teaching since 1983. I would like to thank them here.

My contribution in this book will be the description of a number of structures in the human energy fields with the aim of facilitating a differentiated observation and interpretation of what we can perceive with ourselves and with the other person. For that purpose we / you have to undertake this research 'from the first person' perspective - that is including ourselves. This is both a path of initiation, a path of developing consciousness. I will endeavour to describe this path. In doing so I am expanding the notion of 'personal' development to an understanding of how this is linked automatically to the development of all sentient beings as well as to our planet as a whole.

The essential part of this book will concentrate upon the mental framework required in order to develop Spiritual Healing. In this book I am purposely only proposing a few techniques for working with the hands in the energy fields because we need to strengthen our intuitive right brain. Techniques mainly involve the left hemisphere of the brain (see appendix on the hemispheres of the brain). The techniques that I am proposing and that I feel are necessary, concern meditation and centring in order to be able to work from a place of silence within. This progressive connection to silence allows the right brain, your feelings, and your intuition to develop and gradually open up to non-physical realms. It may also lead to an opening for highly evolved non-physical entities to guide you and work through you. Bob Moore's teaching developed this balanced approach to Spiritual Healing. The Tibetan Buddhist approach is close to his teachings.

In this context I am very happy to refer to the Dalaï Lama's excellent book 'The Universe in a single Atom'. It is evident that Tibetan Buddhism has developed an understanding of great depth concerning first person inquiry, the exploration of consciousness and the techniques required. I am pleased to be able to complement my thoughts with those brought forward in the books of Helen Gamborg 'The Essential is Invisible' as well as Jim Gilkeson's book 'Energy Healing'. Both authors studied with Bob Moore. Bob approved of Helen Gamborg's book many years ago. Other very valuable sources are the various transcriptions of Bob's courses. Most of these have not been published. I am especially grateful to Antje Martin's for her immense work of gathering the transcriptions of Bob's courses from the early 80's. I will also be referring to my previous books in order not to repeat myself unnecessarily.

Beyond magnetism and the purely medical
Spiritual Healing is different from what one would normally call magnetism or mesmerism. The magnetic healer, in the sense that this expression came to be used, in the 19th century, would mainly work on an etheric level. He would use his magnetism (his etheric energy) for doing so. In this strict sense he would not consciously use other levels of energy like the astral, mental or spiritual. If in reality this or that magnetic

healer would also use these other layers of the aura, this would only depend on his personal approach. He could very well see himself as a 'simple' magnetic healer although he was using mental and spiritual energy as well. Strictly speaking though, the work on the etheric alone can have quite spectacular and often immediate effects. However these effects might not last very long, because the deeper causes of a problem are mostly not located in the etheric. Patients can often visit a healer who works on the etheric level for the relief of their physical pains, even if it is only a temporary relief, in much the same way as they would visit a medical doctor. They often have to return to the healer on a regular basis for the relief of their symptom. They may not necessarily be interested in the deeper causes of their pain nor be aware that another approach could bring lasting relief.

During menstruation back pain can be sometimes unbearable. This pain can often be spectacularly relieved when worked on etherically. If the causes are not dealt with, the pain will reappear with the next menstruation. The woman will generally need to return to see a magnetic healer – or ask her husband to put his hands where she feels the pain. Working with our hands and with energy is natural and can be done by everyone, especially this kind of healing.

Spiritual healing in contrast to etheric or magnetic healing does not primarily aim at healing physical pain. Healing is therefore not defined as being a medical treatment or being in competition with the medical profession. Some healers I know will not see individual clients for long unless they get involved in personal development.

The problem with magnetic healing, just as with medical doctors, is that the patient is not usually aware of the need to make any effort to change anything concerning their way of thinking, living or eating. In some way they expect the practitioner and his 'pill' to do everything for them. Although this abdication of responsibility for one's own health is gradually evolving, it has until recently been a prevailing belief in our culture. Spiritual healing works on a spiritual level and aims at clearing the primary causes of a disharmony – that is the separation from our divine nature/ source. Essentially one might say that spiritual healing is not trying to save the body, but rather the soul.

As a healer all we can strive for is to increase the strength of energy that we can bring to a person. This strength is the energy of love. We thus need to discover what love energy consists of and how we can increase our contact with it. The aim of this book is to present a process of freeing our energy system from its restrictions so that we can restore the link with higher consciousness or the divine love energy, with the aim of letting it flow through our system without hindrances. The scientific aspect of spiritual healing helps us to link our consciousness to this process and brings hopefully more precision to our healing work.

The origins and sources of my approach
I have a few thoughts concerning the sources that Bob Moore has used. It is obvious that he received teachings and had numerous meetings with healers from the English tradition. The English healing tradition must have a very old branch (Druidic or Shamanic type) as well as more recent contributions coming from India via the British colonial occupation (Theosophical Society) Bob Moore possibly got the inspiration for his 'science of the triangles' from authors like Alice Bailey who mentioned this. As far as I now she did not develop this science herself. She also mentions the 21 secondary chakras,

which was common knowledge in Indian Yogic Science. Bob explained that his work was coming essentially from three sources: Tibetan and the connection to **discipline**, Egyptian and the link to **precision** and Christianity and the connection to **love**. He also said that he got most of the exercises he was passing on during deep meditation and that they came from an ancient teaching that would surface from time to time throughout history. He did not give more details about this. I am convinced that he had read authors like Edgar Cayce, Harry Edwards, Krishnamurti or 'The Cloud of Unknowing' without them having given the main strands of his teachings. I seem to remember that he had seen a treaty on the Chinese super-meridians in the beginning of the eighties, which probably inspired him to develop his eight psychic streams. His liver stream is very similar but not identical to the Chinese Dai Mai meridian.

Bob was an extraordinarily gifted clairvoyant, he saw the energy fields around the human body in great detail, as well as being able to see the effects of his psycho-energetic exercises. He could observe this directly in the many groups that he taught, each group having up to 40 participants. He has also been my main 'music teacher' since he also worked extensively with the effects of sound. He often used carefully chosen music and could then see its effects upon the people in the room. He knew for instance the effect that would be created by a specific instrument and that it would be beneficial after a particular exercise which was working on the same area of the body. Bob probably worked with about 2,000 students who studied with him between1975-99, some staying for more than twenty years. We all witnessed Bob's precise and very detailed comments after an exercise, an itch here, a sudden pain there or a pressure on a third area. He would launch into lengthy explanations about a person's experiences during an exercise or meditation. At first sight these experiences may have seemed banal, but through his intuitive commentary we learned that they were in fact giving a deep insight into a person's process. Each sensation, each observation during an exercise had a meaning and was linked to our history, our inner process and our present state. His understanding was always so fascinating to hear.

I'm aware of the fact that Bob Moore himself never wanted to write a book on this subject, or on any subject in fact. He was convinced that his teaching could not be faithfully transmitted through books. To transmit this science of Spiritual Healing is rather like wanting to study a large ocean steamer with ten decks and nuclear propulsion by just reading a manual. The field is so vast that when Bob, for a very short period thought he would write about it, he was talking about 12 volumes. However, he quickly dropped the idea, convinced that it was more appropriate to pass on his teaching orally. In 1992 Anna and Alex Mauthner published a rare series of interviews with Bob in a small book 'Conversations with Bob Moore'.

It is true that our culture tends towards fast-food and this is also the case when it comes to spiritual teachings. We need to bear this in mind when working with a book on the subject. A book may seem to serve us everything about a subject so that we could even rush to the last page in order to avoid reading it all, and thus obtain the ultimate key in one night's reading.

I feel that the subject of Spiritual Healing lends itself, only in a very limited way, to be understood through books. Often different authors also seem to be contradicting each other. This can be for various reasons. It may be the case that the author does not write from his or her own experience and is simply quoting other books. They themselves may not have explored what they are writing about. Sadly this is how mistakes and misunderstandings have been passed on from author to author, from generation to generation. We will illustrate this later on by taking the example of where to place the root chakra.

There is also another reason. Quantum physics, like Tibetan Buddhism, teach us that the observer has a considerable influence on what is observed. Thus apparent contradictions may just be different ways of seeing the same object. In the same way if you place an apple in the middle of a circle of people, each person will see and describe it in a slightly different way although it is still the same apple. Helen Gamborg explains this in her book by telling the story of a group of observers who try to describe an elephant in a dark room - they had never seen one before. Depending from where they approached the animal, one would report an animal consisting of a large trunk, another of a single enormous foot, or a huge tusk, etc.

These apparent contradictions oblige us to learn about energy through exploration, and through our own experience. There is really no other way. Contradictions are thus very useful. There is also another difficulty: a description can be taken out of an experienced context and will thus become inexact and lifeless. It is difficult enough to find the right words to describe subtle phenomena or inner experiences. There is also the fact that energy is constantly in movement. We should also not forget that it is not easy to draw energy structures accurately or even to describe them in words.

The reason though for writing this 'impossible' book is to encourage anyone who wishes to travel down the path of

Spiritual Healing, to help them to clarify their approach and to find a way to develop a coherent understanding of what they observe. This can take many years and there is no shortcut. I realise that writing and thinking about this subject is allowing me to clarify my own thoughts and intuitions. I have been studying this fascinating subject for over 35 years. Certain questions have stayed with me sometimes for ten or twenty years before accumulating enough experience and insight to be able to formulate an answer. I sincerely wish that this will benefit students and readers who are studying Spiritual Healing.

The longer I walk upon this path of healing the more I realise that deep healing always happens in co-operation with the spiritual world.

"Healing requires patience, perseverance, persistence and faith."

Dr. Augusto de Almeida,
channelled though Eva Høffding

The method

How can we talk about science when the object of our research cannot be measured? In order to understand the approach we are undertaking – that many others have done before us – we need to understand the notion of what an integrated science is. This science is integrating the left and the right hemispheres of the brain (see appendix), the measurable physical aspects but also the non-physical aspects connected to energy which are obviously not measurable. We are also integrating some aspects of quantum physics. The right brain explores phenomena through direct experience. This produces an experienced and felt knowledge, rather than an intellectual knowledge. The observed object becomes part of our experience. We can feel its true nature and all that is connected with it.

For centuries Western science has obviously made enormous progress in concentrating upon the measurable aspects of phenomena, on analysing and trying to grasp the world intellectually. However this approach has reached its limits. On one hand many of these limits and categories have been challenged by Quantum Physics, that has opened up new dimensions and given birth to theories which we have been trying to come to terms with during the last fifty years. On the other hand western science does not have real answers to some essential questions, for instance to the healing of and the causes of illnesses such as cancer, multiple sclerosis, Altzheimer's disease, and many others. Not knowing the real cause of such illnesses the medical profession seems to grope in the dark and the treatments proposed can often seem like shooting with cannons at what might only be a sparrow. The state of the world today and the numerous cul-de-sacs we encounter seem to be pushing us to open our minds and widen our horizons. We somehow know that we need to open up to new solutions in many areas, and this includes the field of illness and spiritual development.

Scientific methods that integrate left and right brain

The essence of Spiritual Healing resides in consciousness in a wide sense. This study is directed towards subtle phenomena in the field of energy. The methods of investigation need to be conceived especially for this purpose, not unlike the new instruments and methods that were needed in order to investigate the nuclear and cellular worlds. Subtle phenomena can (for the time being) not be measured in a satisfactory way. I can to a certain extent measure the width of an energy field in combining a tape measurer with my observation (a sensitive hand, sight of a clairvoyant, a resonating music instrument like a Tibetan bowl, or the INES – see for the description my book 'Sound healing with the five elements'). Numerous energy phenomena though cannot be measured in this way. In Neuroscience you can observe which part of the brain is active, which 'little lamp is flashing', but we don't know why it does this, nor do we understand how it gets from the 'flash' to, for instance, the vision it creates or why a particular inner image makes a neuron in the brain 'flare up'. Any deeper investigation of such phenomena has then got to refer to inner experience, to consciousness. Here we can certainly learn from the wisdom of the ancient Tibetan tradition as well as from Bob Moore's research.

The potential of the right hemisphere of the brain
In 2006 during the Biosynthesis Congress in Lisbon the American Neuro-psychologist Allan Schore brilliantly explained the immense and mainly hidden resources of the right hemisphere of the brain. Neurosciences have discovered that our right brain perceives a wealth of information, that we are not conscious of, but that our body reacts to, for instance by sending out hormones. "Current interest (in Neuroscience includes) right brain systems involved in non-conscious processing of emotion." Allan Schore. He also quoted Decety and Chaminade (*Consciousness and Cognition*, 2003): "Self awareness, empathy, identification with others, and more generally inter-subjective processes, are largely dependent upon right hemisphere resources." Allan Schore : "The therapist is also listening and interacting at another level, an intuitive, experience-near *subjective level*, one that implicitly processes moment-to-moment socio-emotional information at levels beneath awareness."

"Just as the left brain communicates its states to other left brains via conscious linguistic behaviours so the right brain non- verbally communicates its unconscious states to other right brains *that are tuned to receive these communications*." (Schore, 2003) "The left hemisphere is more involved in the foreground-analytic (conscious) processing of information, whereas the right hemisphere is more involved in the background-holistic (subconscious) processing of information." (Prodan et al., 2001).

A healer or a teacher is not separate from a patient or a student. This explains partly why we can transmit energy over a distance. Numerous experiments, especially in quantum physics have given evidence for this where a twin particle brought to the other side of the world is still reacting when something happens to its twin.

We can very well imagine that it is just a matter of time before somebody will invent a device that will be able, at least partially, to detect and measure energy. Kirlian photography has gone some way with this, even though they measure much less than they would like to. In my understanding Kirlian photography or similar devices mainly perceive a part of the etheric energy field, probably the area one calls the health aura. There is much more to energy than that.

In working with the subtle effects of sound (see my previous books) I have come across several musical instruments, with a fairly stable sound (tuning forks, INES, singing bowls) that make the borders of the energy field audible. Their sound and especially a part of the overtone spectrum (the colour of their sound) is then absorbed when it goes through dense areas of the aura or meets the border of the energy field. In other places the sound becomes more brilliant, audibly so for everyone present in the room. However these instruments reveal a flood of information about energy structures in a room or around a person, which we are then left to interpret. The fact of being able to thus observe energy structures objectively helps our mind to grasp and then share objective information with other people.

From here it is easy to imagine that one might be able to link a microphone and a camera to some software that would allow one to record variations of overtones and amplitude, connected to the movement of a sounding object in the energy field, as described above, and then show this three dimensionally on a computer screen. Energy structures would then become visible for people who are not naturally clairvoyant. Although such an experiment would probably only show a very limited spectrum of energy, it would nevertheless be very helpful.

Consciousness as a tool

The Dalaï Lama gives us a beautiful introduction to this subject in his book 'The Universe in a Single Atom': "A crucial point about the study of consciousness, as opposed to the study of the physical world, relates to the personal perspective of accounts like this." (p. 133) And a little further down on that page: "What is required, if science is successfully to probe the nature of consciousness, is nothing short of a paradigm shift. That is, the third-person perspective, which can measure phenomena from the point of view of an independent observer, must be integrated with a first person perspective, which will allow the incorporation of subjectivity and the qualities that characterize the experience of consciousness." "Given that one of the primary characteristics of consciousness is the subjective and experiential nature, any systematic study of it must adopt a method that will give access to the dimensions of subjectivity and experience."

A Comprehensive scientific study of consciousness must therefore embrace both third-person and first-person methods: it cannot ignore the phenomenological reality of subjective experience but must observe all the rules of scientific rigor. " (p. 134; for the definitions of 'mind' and 'consciousness' see appendix)

The method of investigation from the first-person perspective

The Dalaï Lama: "Whether we talk of the transformation of consciousness or of the introspective empirical analysis of what occurs in the mind, the observer needs a range of skills, carefully honed through repetition and training, and applied in a rigorous and disciplined manner. All these practices assume a certain ability to direct one's mind to a chosen object and to hold the attention there for a period, however brief." (p. 150)

It is true that the insight into profound experience shared in his book gives us precious indications as to how to proceed in an investigation from the first person.

Consciousness allows us to explore objects, for instance a secondary chakra, energy points or accumulations of energy. In order to do this we combine our intention with our feelings. The intention mentally defines the object we are going to explore (left analytical brain) before we begin the exploration: exact location of the energy points e.g. or where exactly we are going to draw a line on the skin surface along which our feelings are going to move and observe. The intention is also going to define the form of attention we are going to use: for instance an overall awareness, that of moving along a line very slowly towards a precise point. Our intention will also give us a protocol of research that will indicate to us how to proceed should we meet certain phenomena or obstacles such as sleepiness, doubt or other emotions, the interior radio or busy mind, loosing our track altogether, or switching temporarily onto another level of consciousness. This protocol will tell us for instance whether we need to start all over again at the beginning or to go back and forth for a while in the zone where we met the difficulty or lack of clarity. In the triangle exercise (see below) we are using for instance a line that we want to follow on the skin surface and not move away from. We shall explain the reason why.

In the triangle exercise described below we need to move our awareness along a line or towards a point slowly, and observe the following:

- not to force when meeting resistance,
- memorising all we can.
- to write down our observations at the end of the exercise.
- to repeat the exercise regularly over a period of time.

These observations can concern the period of time when we do the exercise but also the 36 hours following it (including the dreams at night). We will also try to observe possible changes in our habitual ways of thinking or functioning in our daily life.

In a second phase the study of the energy structures gives us paths of reflection that help us to interpret our observations. Our feelings will then provide valuable information as to the exactness of our possible interpretations. Certain interpretations can however take month or even years, in some extreme cases. This method of fine tuned feeling-observation in the first person thus consists of two phases: observation and experience with the subsequent taking of notes. Subsequent to this is the phase of interpretation, which sometimes can require an experienced/intuitive third person to give us suggestions as to how to interpret the experience we have had during the exercise.

In the field of Spiritual Healing and human growth it is not very helpful to remain on a theoretical level. If there is wisdom, then it can only be wisdom acquired through feeling and personal experience of the observer – that is us. This is the precise challenge and beauty of this method. It is however diametrically opposed to the western scientific approach, with the exception of Quantum Physics that has discovered that the results of an experiment differ according to what the observer has set out to observe. The nuclear physicist can for instance either discover where an electron is but then cannot measure its speed, or he can decide to measure the speed but will not know where the electron is.

For many years the prevailing belief of most Western scientists is that they think that an object can be observed without the observer having an influence on it. They therefore think that an observer can be replaced by another and that they will still get the same result. This works well in certain fields (like Newtonian physics) and can be a complete illusion in others. Treating a person's energy fields (whether this is done with the consciousness of these energy fields or not) is such an example. In fact, I believe that during a treatment the energy fields of the medical doctor, practitioner or healer and the patient's will always be influencing each other. It is therefore useful to learn to observe as objectively as possible what is going on. See the chapter on the 'Process', paragraph on meditation.

Discerning real from illusion
The primary objective in exploring energy in this way is to avoid illusions or at least recognise them as such. This requires precise tools that allow us to discern the difference between impressions that have their origin in our emotions or are attracted by them, and information that is coming from non-emotional and objective awareness on the other hand. In my courses we spend three quarter of the time learning through practice, experience and sharing, which includes all aspects of feeling, subtle perception and intuition.

In order to develop our awareness and intuition so that they become trustworthy tools, it is necessary to work with the transformation of our own energy. It is only through this process that we become aware of our shadows and blind spots. Knowing ourselves better is the only way to learn how to make this difference.

We must remember that our solar plexus is linked to the sense of sight and also to the astral and therefore it can easily create illusions. Disciplined and sincere work on our subconscious allows our faculty of discernment to become more stable and trustworthy.

The Dalaï Lama: "Even when combined, neuroscience and behavioural psychology do not shed enough light on the subjective experience, as both approaches still place primary importance on the objective, third-person perspective. Contemplative traditions on the whole have historically emphasized subjective, first-person investigation of the nature and functions of consciousness, by training the mind to focus in a disciplined way on its own internal states.'

In this kind of analysis the observer, the object, and the means of investigation are all aspects of the same thing, namely the mind of the individual experimenter. In Buddhism, this mental training is called *bhavana* (or *gom* in Tibetan), which is usually translated as 'meditation' in English. (p. 141) And a bit further on: "People often understand *meditation* to refer simply to an emptying of the mind, or a relaxation practice, but that is not what I mean here. The practice of *gom* does not imply any mysterious or mystical state of ecstasy open only to a few gifted individuals. The term *gom* refers both to a means, or a process, and to a state that may arise as a result of the process. I am concerned here primarily with *gom* as a means, which implies a rigorous, focused, and disciplined use of introspection and mindfulness to probe deeply into the nature of a chosen object. From the scientific point of view, this process can be compared with rigorous empirical observation." (p. 142)

All Buddhist schools of meditation training in the observation of consciousness have developed tools for perfecting the mind. They have all detected **the five major obstacles** to an untrained mind: doubt, sleepiness, agitation, impatience or anger and the lack of alertness.

Observing the non-visible
We must also train ourselves to open our mind to our object of investigation that is not visible to normal sight. This type of observation depends largely on the object that our mind places at the centre of its attention. It is an investigation of the mind by the mind where we must learn to recognise our own programs of self-censoring. The French say: 'Nobody is deafer than the one who does not want to hear.' If we don't want to believe in something, than we wont see it. This is even truer for the non-visible dimensions.

I remember two little stories that Bob told us. The first was about the faculty of being able to see energy fields around a person on a television screen. For years he had been convinced that this was not possible. Until the day he decided: 'Why not, after all. Let's try.' From that moment on he could see energy fields on the television as if the people were in the room. One day I asked him if he could see the Chinese acupuncture meridians. He answered: 'To be perfectly honest, I have never seen anything like that.' This simply meant that his field of interest and investigation was not directed towards these aspects. He was working with the eight psychic streams and therefore saw those. We will talk about them further on. The fact of writing this book allows me not only to formulate the state of my research and understanding but also, I hope, help the reader to more easily focus on these aspects and through that to learn to perceive and understand them better.

This question of focussing is very interesting. In her book 'A summer with the Leprachauns' Tanis Helliwell describes a number of dialogues with a Leprachaun on Achill Island in Ireland. This being explains to her that he had a meeting with Rudolf Steiner (amazing !) at the beginning of the twentieth century. Steiner had explained to him that it was necessary for nature elementals and human beings start to communicate and co-operate in order to aid the evolution of the earth. For that purpose humans had to learn to develop a more subtle and diffuse perception (right brain), leading them towards the perception of energy, including feelings. The nature elementals, like the leprechaun, had to learn to be more focussed at times. This would lower their frequency and make them denser and thus closer to the physical world for the length of a conversation with humans. The etheric world, where these elementals live, is – as described in fairy tales and legends – more vague, dreamy and misty.

These interviews with nature spirits are very serious and seem only to have become possible after about 1995, when the spirit of our time seems to have changed, making way for a more scientific approach of these worlds.

The exercises that we proposed in previous books and in this one allow us to enter the etheric perception of the world and more specifically the energy dimensions beyond the four layers of the etheric.

Daniel Perret – The Science of Spiritual Healing

Bob Moore worked very much in this scientific way. He had the capacity to teach the position of a number of energy points and structures in our own system with enormous precision. He also taught us how to direct our attention to our own experiences of these points and structures.

This frame of personal experience, of felt knowledge is essential. It becomes possible when the left brain (localising the structures and focussing on the main subjects of their links and story) starts to cooperate with the right hemisphere of the brain (feeling, multi- dimensional experience including subtle and non-visible aspects). This approach takes the feeling dimension out of an esoteric and mystical connotation and brings it into our concrete experience. This is a considerable step.

The means of observing energy or the non-visible are for instance

- A stable sounding instrument, as described above
- Seeing energy objectively (clairvoyant, objective view), this to a more or lesser degree.
- Seeing energy with in inner vision (subjective view), that is with closed eyes.
- Feeling energy with our hands or
- Hearing energy or
- Smelling energy.
- There is also, what I call, auric perception where my energy field seems to extend and surround the object of my investigation. I can then see/feel energy structures. I don't see them as such with my eyes, but I know with certainty where there is an energy structure. I can for instance feel/see the place of an energy blockage in a person's back while the person is facing

me. I cannot see her back directly. My eyes work as a means of focussing in space rather than for directly seeing the energy.

The triangle exercise

We will now describe an exercise that uses a geometrical structure - a triangle with two equal sides which is a stable geometrical figure. Our left brain, the intellect, allows us to establish in advance where to draw a line that will link up three points on the body, starting in this case at the third eye (chakra on the forehead), then moving down, on the skin surface, along the right arm to the secondary chakra in the right hand. We then move through the air to reach the same spot on the left hand, move up the left arm on skin surface and back to the third eye. (For the exact locations of these points see the diagram further down). Our right brain, that is our feeling perception, allows us to experience a number of invisible dimensions: emotions, thoughts, memories, images, etc. On one hand we have the logical well defined path of the line, anchored in our mental intention, on the other hand we have our feeling observation in all its facets. How successful our observation will be depends upon the quality of quite a slow movement along the skin surface.

This way of working allows us to observe a well defined zone with great precision. We will know that we are getting a good contact with it when we start feeling differences (between left and right arm or hand, beginning, middle or end of a arm line, one point compared to the other, etc.) The other thing that tells us that our observation is successful is paradoxically linked to feeling obstacles. These can hinder our attention considerably up to the point of loosing the contact with what we are doing. At this point we'll know that we have entered an etheric perception.

Daniel Perret – The Science of Spiritual Healing

Experiencing the etheric field

In the beginning this experience may be surprising, because we cannot compare it with anything we have known before. While slowly drawing our lines on the skin surface, as suggested in the exercise, all seems to go well in the beginning. We get used to this intense and minute observation, because of how slowly we are moving along the line and observing. Then suddenly it can happen that our awareness gets stuck and we feel it is impossible to move on. We can meet a kind of fog, an unusual stickiness or slowness, a strong sense of sleepiness or suddenly wanting to think about something else. That is if we can manage to keep an uninterrupted awareness of what we are doing. The slow pace of our progression along the line, allows us to connect to precise information about our body/energy during this observation.

This is a process where we meet and progressively dissolve resistances. It is these resistances that obscure our perception and make us surf superficially along the chosen line of observation. We can at times loose our awareness of what we are doing altogether and may not even remember where we were on the triangle. Then we will need to start again at the beginning point. It also can happen that we switch involuntarily to another plane of consciousness. This can manifest itself through an image or suddenly being in a scene we may or may not know. All this can happen in a split second after which we sort of 'wake up' again and realise we had been gone for a length of time and possibly lost the memory of where we were in the exercise. This is all information that is contained in the etheric and which now enters our consciousness.

There are a number of other phenomena that can happen. The line might want to move around an invisible obstacle and avoid continuing on the planned path. The line can also jump and want to leave the skin surface. That can happen when there is a split between the inner and the outer etheric, the life and light ether.

This simple exercise is actually starting a number of processes. On one hand discovering obstacles or differences allows our mind to bring into consciousness some aspects of a blockage (emotions, thoughts, memories, etc.). The chosen geometrical form will of itself produce a stabilising effect (balance). The hands become linked to a higher level of consciousness through the connection with the third eye chakra. Then two aspects of polarity are being balanced (left, right; feminine and masculine and the different levels of our expression through our hands). The fact of drawing a line on the skin surface along our arms contributes to healing the connection between the inner and outer etheric. We shall explain this in more detail later on. The split between the inner and outer etheric is brought about by a division between feeling and expression which can be linked to a lack of honesty.

The understanding of the experience can help but is not always necessary for the exercise to work. We cannot though focus on an interpretation during this exercise since the left brain would take over and interrupt the conscious perception of the right brain. The interpretation can take place just after the exercise, but often will continue for hours, days and sometimes weeks. An exercise, as the word indicates, needs to be practised over a period of time and with discipline if one wants to be able to link the experience at the time of doing the exercise with the long term results that it brings. For an exercise like this we usually need about10 to 15 minutes. With 'usually' I mean, when we are not too stressed and do not need to do some grounding, breathing or relaxation beforehand. Discipline is the key to felt knowledge. If you do this exercise just once or twice or with long spaces in between you will not have the means to understand its potential and above all to be able to observe the effects on yourself. Then the exercise and its transmission won't work. When you do an exercise like this for the first time you need to keep doing it for at least a two month period. (See diagram page 54)

The energy structures

Before we explain the subtle anatomy we should remember the basic axiom in Tibetan Buddhism which is impermanence. All energy is constantly in movement and to try to draw it and thus to freeze it in a certain position is a simplification and fundamentally inexact. We need to remember this whilst reading this section and looking at the diagrams. There are energy structures that have a tendency to remain more stable, like the belief streams, the rim of the mental aura, the vertical streams, the major chakras, and the position of the secondary chakras. On the other hand we have the etheric that is in constant movement. The same is true for most of the mental aura. When I try to describe structures it is in order to use them as reference points and to be able to discern their differences. This contributes to the precision of the work on ourselves and with others. The structures that we can see in the human energy fields are : lines, points, crosses, triangles, squares and circles – the basic forms of geometry.

When we describe the various energy structures, we must remember that they are not merely crossings of energy lines but that these structures also connect each individual to his history and to a number of levels of consciousness: emotions, thoughts, memories, spiritual aspects, etc.

Energy Points
Bob: "When you look at points in the aura, they have a tremendous meaning. Lines of energy coming together produce a point, that is at the intersection of what the lines are doing. Within that intersection there is strength. When you

come to look at the aura structure you don't see lines as such but what you are seeing is more points. These points are the strength of the energy being drawn from different directions and so producing the relationship of, say, vertical energy to horizontal energy and so you have the strength showing in a point or a number of points. Some points of course have more strength than others because you have more directions of energy drawn to the point."

"The points that we see energy being drawn towards and energy moving from, those points produce an activity of energy. That activity of energy is possibly not moving as it should move, it is trapped. Perhaps you have got a lot of emotion there, self-pity; perhaps you have built in a strong area of your personality. So when we come to use such points then one point has got to reflect to another point and so we start a circulation and that circulation begins a process of change and so when we come to use thoughts with points we come into something that is tremendously strong, active, vibrant, producing a change. Of course that change doesn't work with everyone, it takes time and so some people have to go through more change than others, some have to release some emotional attachments to things that they have been doing… (in life)."

"So points that we use will reflect such effects and so you can find that all aspects of your life show up within these changes, not just working with an exercise, but everything that you are doing in your life has got to come into contact with that change… So development, working with energy, using our thoughts, will take its effect in every aspect of your life, there is NO SEPARATION. You cannot look at this as something that is connected to just one aspect, everything that you are doing will be affected by working with those points."

Daniel Perret – The Science of Spiritual Healing

Energy fields

*The etheric, astral, mental, causal (karma),
'spiritual' levels and beyond*

The physical human body is surrounded by energy fields which each have different vibratory levels. **The etheric** is closest to the body and has a comparatively dense energy. You can sense the outer layer starting at about 25 cm from the skin surface (see illustration p. 38). We will explain the etheric level in more detail below.

The next level beyond the etheric is the **astral or emotional aura**. This field has got two parts. Closer to the body, next to the etheric, we find the lower, denser astral with its painful emotions such as hate, jealousy, fear, etc. These emotions can be felt as denseness in the aura and are generally linked to an area of the physical body and to the etheric, as well as to an area in the mental aura (containing thought structures). The astral has a tendency to resist all changes. In other words we have, as we know, a hard time getting rid of emotional habits.

The upper astral extends from the lower astral up to the causal aura and contains our transformed emotions, that is, our feelings like compassion, love, serenity, etc. Just inside the spiritual layer of the aura we can find the **causal aura**, containing the karmic causes or deeper causes of disharmony in this life.

Around our head we have the **mental aura**. The mental energy field stores our thoughts, including thought structures that have been affected by an accident or a shock. The mental energy field reflects and conditions what happens in the brain. Some aspects of stress connected to intellectual thinking (often caused by emotional infiltration) can be detected close to the left hemisphere of the brain, and dispersed by working there in the aura structure. The mental energy field, when at rest, forms a bowl around the head that we can see represented in many orthodox icons or Buddhist paintings. This rim of the mental aura reaches to just below the heart chakra and comes into the body at the shoulder polarity points. We can feel this rim quite easily with our hands. It is the place where the mental activity withdraws when it is not active. Perception and interpretation of what is happening in the mental aura depends on how far we have developed the use of the third eye, because the activity in the mental aura is very fast. We may sometimes perceive an image or a rapid succession of images. The upper mental is roughly situated above our belief streams, ears and eyebrows and stores clear thoughts, less infiltrated by emotions and would contain symbols, abstract and universal thoughts, and intuitions. The lower mental (below the belief streams) is infiltrated by our emotions and is where lot of our intellectual activity takes place.

The **causal aura** contains the karmic causes and strong emotional imprints from this life that have created karmic debts. This layer is not very wide and can be found just inside the spiritual aura.

At arms length we find the **spiritual part of the aura**. This part contains our inborn spiritual qualities (see p. 93).

The links between the different places where memories are stored are mostly unconscious. They can however be activated, sometimes through meeting similar situations in our daily lives or through meditation, awareness exercises, spontaneous creative expression, reflecting upon the event, talking about it and getting more clarity. The links then become increasingly conscious.

The human energy fields do not stop at the spiritual aura. I have observed three more **layers beyond** this, each one about a foot away from each other. I have a limited experience of these levels and at this time my feeling is that we can essentially work with prayer in those areas.

The successive layers of the aura reflect the path of our development process from the physical-etheric consciousness through the transformation of the lower astral into feeling. This acquired softness helps to clear our karmic structures before we, so to speak, get an unhindered access to our spiritual qualities. This then creates a more permanent movement from the spiritual aura into the body and back.

Our Energy fields

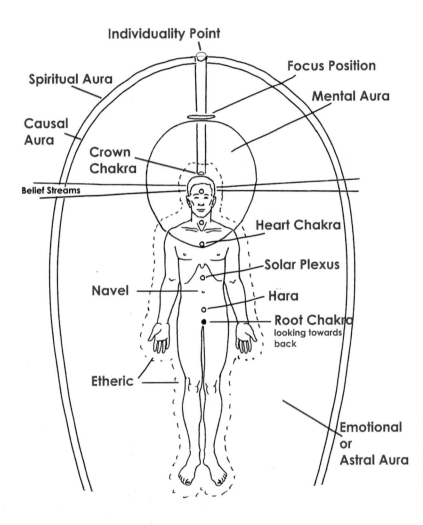

Individuality Point

Focus Position

Spiritual Aura

Mental Aura

Causal Aura

Crown Chakra

Belief Streams

Heart Chakra

Solar Plexus

Navel

Hara

Root Chakra
looking towards back

Etheric

Emotional or Astral Aura

The spine and its correspondences

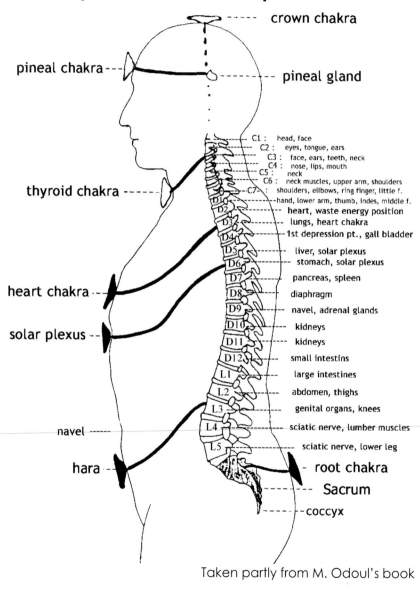

crown chakra

pineal chakra

pineal gland

C1 : head, face
C2 : eyes, tongue, ears
C3 : face, ears, teeth, neck
C4 : nose, lips, mouth
C5 : neck
C6 : neck muscles, upper arm, shoulders
C7 : shoulders, ellbows, ring finger, little f.

thyroid chakra

hand, lower arm, thumb, indes, middle f.
heart, waste energy position
lungs, heart chakra
1st depression pt., gall bladder

liver, solar plexus
stomach, solar plexus

pancreas, spleen

heart chakra

diaphragm

navel, adrenal glands

solar plexus

kidneys
kidneys

small intestins

large intestines

abdomen, thighs

genital organs, knees

navel

sciatic nerve, lumber muscles

sciatic nerve, lower leg

hara

root chakra

Sacrum

coccyx

Taken partly from M. Odoul's book

Daniel Perret – The Science of Spiritual Healing

Prana Energy

The vital energy - known as prana in India, chi in China, bio energy or life force energy by others - comes from the sun and is composed of infra-red, ultra-violet, electricity, heat and solar light. This energy enters our system at the etheric spleen and is subsequently distributed towards the major chakras. From there the energy is distributed to the 21 secondary chakras and the other energy points using a network of energy lines. Then the energy reaches the autonomous nervous system, the endocrine glands and through their hormones finally reaches the blood.

Distribution of prana energy

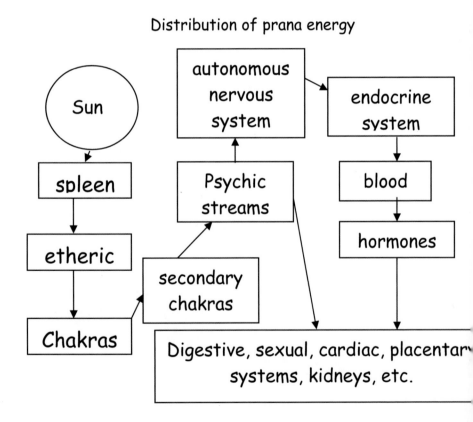

The Etheric

The etheric is an intersection of different energies from very fast moving energy, like intuition, higher consciousness energy and slower energy like the physical body or the energy of the astral and mental. All experience is stored in the etheric. The function of the etheric is to store energy that can then be used for various activities, like running.

The four layers of the etheric

Chemical, light, life and reflector ethers

The two first layers are inside the physical body and are separated from the two layers outside the body at the level of the physical skin. You can sense the two outer ones quite easily as being like the layers of a cream cake. The reflector ether starts at about 25 cm from the skin surface, the life ether at about 10 cm. The distance depends on how relaxed the person is in general in a particular area of the body. I cannot say how the two layers inside the body are positioned. Bob explained that the four layers were interlaced. He said that certain points, like the secondary chakras, the 1st depression point or the four polarity points (shoulders, hip bone points) had a connection to all four layers whereas some points in the lower part of the torso mainly had a link to the chemical ether, due to the fact that they are in charge of elimination (digestion, menstruation). The etheric has got the densest energy of all our energy fields and vibrates at a much lower frequency than the astral, mental or spiritual layers. The life ether feels denser to me than the reflector ether.

The etheric plays an important role in the integration of the different energy layers and levels of consciousness. It takes care of an overall circulation of energy from head to toes and brings pranic energy from outside to finally reach the cells of our body with the help of the chemical ether. On a consciousness level this process corresponds to letting external experiences in so that they get 'under our skin' and then to become aware of how they feel deep inside. In a natural state this would trigger a true reaction from our part which we would then ideally express outwards.

Bob: "We often keep an experience outside. When we progress, we let the experience get inside us."

This process is interrupted when on one hand we don't let external experiences in, and on the other hand when we don't express what we feel about those experiences. This then creates a split between the etheric inside and the etheric outside the body, between the truth and the life ether. We can look on this as a lack of truth or a lie and this split creates a blockage in us. Alcohol and drugs have the same effect. We can detect such zones when we draw a line on skin surface and go through those places. This example shows us the value of drawing lines like that. Directing mental and feeling energy towards these areas gives us the means to connect to our feelings about an experience that until then we may not have been able to process. Once we reconnect to our feelings, our consciousness then heals the split in our etheric. We become realigned to the truth of our own feelings.

The four layers of the etheric can be found surrounding and penetrating any living organism, the whole earth, plants, trees, an animal or a stone. One layer can be more predominant around certain plants or places.

The etheric stores any impression we get from our senses, without discrimination. It does not have an intelligence like the astral and therefore cannot select what it wants to store or not. Access to stored memory in the etheric as well as to its control can only operate through the mental level. Bob: "The control of etheric storage is only possible through the mind level. The area of control are the 4 upper chakras but centred in the pineal. This control can be interrupted by navel area."

Chemical ether
This is the layer deepest inside the body and is linked to the element of water, to sound, colour and numbers. The link with numbers can be directly seen in the periodic table of the chemical elements (Mendeleïev). The chemical ether is responsible for the nourishment of the bones, muscles, cells and organs. It is linked to the liver, the spleen, metabolism, to the assimilation and elimination of substances not used in digestion. Its symbol is the lower half of a circle or the half moon.

Light ether
This ether is also called the truth ether and is strongly linked to the element of fire as well as to universal structures like light, love and life. Light is essential for healing depression. The light ether is found just under the skin and needs to be vibrant and have a good pulsation. It is very present around the head and especially in the zones linked to thinking. Its symbol is the triangle.

Life ether
This ether is linked to the element of earth and everyday life. It extends about10-12 cm out from the skin surface. It feels denser than the reflector ether. The (daily) life ether co-ordinates/remembers the activities of daily life in as much as it allows us to do certain routine activities almost automatically, without having to think about what we are doing. We can see

this happening when we can drive several hundred meters, on a road we know well, and at the same time think about something completely different. This is possible because the life ether has stored all the information for that specific routine activity many times. The 'daily life' ether reflects the polarity situation between male and female, positive and negative. It is strongly present in the zones of procreation and involved with menstruation and its potential for purification. You find it also predominantly around the female breasts. The life ether plays an important role in our physical health and gradually withdraws when a person reaches the death process. It is connected to how we accept ourselves.

Reflector ether or warmth ether
This layer of the etheric is linked to the element of air and is found furthest away from the skin surface. Its symbol is the circle. Bob: "The reflector attracts what the chemical ether needs. This reflector ether also has the function to reflect towards the exterior what we feel deep inside us. Thoughts from the exterior (e.g. intuitions) penetrate our system here before entering the brain. This layer gives us the means to see colours, to see the aura, to feel the quality of contact between people. It contains also the world memory, wisdom, knowledge, the physical memory." It reflects what higher energies are bringing into the physical and into our thoughts (intuitions, in the heart and chest area).

"The reflector ether is the highest ether, the highest energy contact that you can achieve. In that energy contact you have got all the things that are necessary, you have peace, contentment in yourself, you have your connection with the universe, you have a relationship to light, you have what is drawn from that light into the body through the chemical ether and then you have the balance of life which you will find in the balance with nature and yourself. The reflector ether is reflecting all of that as a combination, but centred really on the peace."

"Everything that is taking place can be reflected outward. So you can use the outer part of the etheric as a means of reflecting out emotion (anger or suchlike) or creating your own projections. That is being done from what you would be retaining within yourself, related to your emotions. There is not necessarily a feed in - to reach that - from a higher level. Maybe you are just projecting out again your own reflections back from other people's emotions. That may mean you are separating the outer layer of the etheric from other layers. So you are just using the outer layer as a reflector backward from what other people are saying to you. You don't want to be hurt so you just throw it back to them again. You are creating a sort of a vicious circle. But that of course is not helpful to the etheric itself nor to the other levels of the etheric which need to be incorporated if you are going to be using say such things as compassion, which is also a reflector."

We can understand that this process of reflecting is vital and is always linked to our expression. The root chakra and the thyroid chakra, are the two main chakras involved in expression, they are strongly linked to the reflector ether and have an important part to play in its movement.

Bob: "The use of these four ethers that we see in the etheric are not just in our etheric, they are also in the etheric around the world. This is why, when we look at the development of any one person, it can never be a singular development, it has got to relate to other people, to the universe."

Daniel Perret – The Science of Spiritual Healing

The Five Elements & their correspondences

	earth	water	fire	air	space
Quality of the element	solid	Liquid	heat, light, warmth	light, invisible, free, flexible	Emptiness
Body zone	feet > sacrum	> heat point, 3 fingers underneath navel	> lower end of sternum	chest	> eye brows
Type of energy	masculine	Feminine	masculine	feminine	unified
Tendency	descending, adhesive	descending gathering	ascending, expanding, ripening	dispersing	dissolving
Symbol	☐	☽	△	○	⊙
Zodiac sign	♉ ♍ ♑	♓ ♋ ♏	♈ ♌ ♐	♒ ♊ ♎	
Tibetan	gives support	Amalgam-mates	amplifies	allows movement	
Chakra	root	Hara	solar plexus	heart	thyroid
Endocrine glands	adrenals	ovaries, testicles	pancreas	thymus	thyroid
Chakra location	sacrum, at back	5 finger below navel	stomach	middle of sternum	throat
Reich's body zones	buttocks	Belly	diaphragm	chest	neck
Sense	smell	taste	sight	touch	hearing
Emotion	insecurity	anger	fear	depression	suppression
Feeling	security	Calm	love, understanding	joy	expression

Quality	stability, concentra-tion	vitality, creativity	Transforma-tion of emotions	inspiration	essence, emptiness
Level	physique	etheric	astral	mental	conscience
Etheric layers	life ether	chemical ether	light ether	reflector/ warmth ether	

Exercise for balancing the etheric on either side of the body
Sit in a north or south corner of a room. Place the side of the body with the better etheric extension towards the wall and the deficient one away from the wall. Observe what happens. 10-15 minutes.

The seven major chakras

Depending on the tradition we can find a varying number of major chakras, normally between five and eight. There are various reasons for this and differences do not mean that one tradition is right and that the others are wrong. The important thing is how we use the chakras in terms of spiritual development.

In our approach we define a major chakra by its potential to be developed and transformed. Energy points, on the contrary, cannot be developed. They can only be expanded in order to link up better with other points and levels of consciousness. This happens through our conscious contact with them. This is different from the main chakras which always have a specific emotional theme and the potential to transform it into its spiritual aspect. The crown chakra is the only exception, in that it cannot directly be developed and its energy is the reflection of the development of the other six major chakras.

We need a clear motivation, discipline and patience in order to link to the themes of one or several chakras and to establish a progressive contact with them. One of the challenges in teaching and writing about chakras is to underline the understanding and the time needed to develop them. That is why we have spent more time on the method of investigation and the process rather than on theoretical knowledge which could only be out of context - out of the context of individual experience. It is not sufficient to sit on a chair or cross legged to do an exercise, taking five or ten minutes with the chakras, and then think we could understand and transform them all. You would be disappointed and doubt would win (see the five hindrances page 18). Of course this depends upon your level of development and upon how much you have done this kind of work in the past. Considering the complexity of levels of consciousness that meet in a chakra and the depth of its theme, it is more realistic to practice patience.

I have been working with chakras for over 35 years. Each one seems to be a 'book' in itself. If we want to understand them we need, in my experience, to read their 'chapters ', that is also work with and understand the secondary chakras and energy points. Needless to say it is an illusion to believe someone could heal or balance all the chakras in a few sessions or weeks. They are the book of our life ...with its seven seals. That is their richness – and our path.

We shall give an overview of the central themes of the major chakras. We aim to give you an idea of the numerous links between them and the themes that these connections are made up of. I invite you to look on the diagram of the 'five elements & their correspondences' and also at my previous books as I will not repeat what I have already written there.

The major chakras are shaped like funnels. Their opening can be found about two centimetres above the skin surface in the etheric and can reach a diameter of approximately 10 -12 centimetres. The funnel then gets smaller, goes into the body and rises up towards the spine (see drawing p. 26). They draw in two kinds of energy: prana energy and spiritual energy. The draw in of energy is referred to as primary energy, the movement out is known as secondary energy. The primary energy moves to the spine where it meets up with the essence stream in the centre of the spine and then moves out again along the funnel. It is this outpouring energy that feeds the whole energy system through the secondary chakras and energy streams. The direction of the circulation of a chakra depends on the level of consciousness you contact with that chakra. There is therefore not a set direction of rotation in any one given chakra. On the etheric level for instance the rotations follows the general direction of the overall etheric flow of the front of the body that is up the left side and down the right side.

Root chakra
The root chakra is responsible for our contact with the ground, with everyday life and the basis of this life: money, housing, partner, our children, work, our sense of security, feeling useful and successful or the opposite to this. Trans-generational and karmic aspects come into this as well. So, there is a strong link to the causal aura.

Being the chakra furthest away from the ID point above our head, spiritual energy, the light aspect, the energy of our soul, has to move through all the chakras, all the resistances and obstacles before finally reaching the root chakra. At the end of the day this becomes – metaphorically speaking – the crystal, the precious stone, the light in the earth. The root chakra has a strong link to the *earth* element.

Once a student asked Bob in a course: "Why is it that after all these years of courses with you we still have to do grounding exercises?" He explained the function of the root chakra adding with his usual humour: "Grounding is something very difficult to achieve. The ultimate grounding, I believe, will take place with our burial." Others have named this process 'incarnation'.

When we read the quotation above, the themes that may need to be healed connected to the root chakra, come to mind. A person who lacked basic security in their early childhood, would have an underlying insecurity within themselves. This can lead to a resistance to life and to a denial of wanting to exist at all.

The root chakra is located at the back in the sacrum, the sacral bone (see drawing). Other traditions have situated it at the perineum point. According to our definition the perineum point is a simple energy point and cannot be developed in the sense that a chakra can. (See perineum point description on p. 47)

Hara chakra
Water is metaphorically speaking the element of the hara. This directly connects us to the essence of life, as life is born from water. It is therefore not astonishing that not only the reproductive organs are in the area of the hara, but also our possibility to be at peace with ourselves and with the world. The hara connects us to our instinctive and natural

intelligence, to respect for our body and for all other beings: plants, animals, humans, other races, nature in general. Harmony, peace of body and mind are possible when we balance the male and female polarity within us. The hara symbol of the horizontal half moon or cup shows us that in its centre there is a resting point of balance for any liquid or marble we put in it. This leads us to understand that a deeper contact with nature spirits and non-physical beings can only be reached when we attain this inner peace of the hara.

Our overly dominant intellect, the fascist tendency in each of us, is often the disturbing element that tries to force its will onto our inner nature. It is the opposite of creativity, and is also met in the hara. You can find the hara chakra about five fingers below the navel (see also my book 'Roots of Musicality').

Solar plexus
"The solar plexus is the graveyard of our good intentions." Bob loved to repeat this. It is truer than we would like to admit. We have mentioned that it is in the solar plexus that the real transformation of our emotions happens. The ultimate aim is to release our fears and to surrender to love as the strongest energy. We can come to an acceptance and to the understanding that everything has a deeper meaning and that we have attracted all the circumstances of our lives. This is not easily achieved. The intellect (through an unbalanced pineal chakra) has a strong influence on the solar plexus. The solar plexus, the chakra with the strongest connection to the astral, is the seat of the ego which is the excessive identification with fears, but it also connects us to light and truth. We experience our painful emotions and all the tricks of the ego defences there.

The meeting and transformation of emotion at the level of the solar plexus is the passage into the field of love. For a person to be utterly convinced that in all circumstances love and compassion is the ultimate solution, perhaps requires a number of lives where they have tried everything else until they finally surrender to love. The solar plexus is situated in the stomach area.

Heart Chakra

Once the energy of the solar plexus is transformed it reaches the heart. Once we have activated and transformed the energy of the lower three chakras, our compassion and joy can finally spread and widen out at the level of the heart. In the heart we need to overcome the trap of self pity, let go of attachment and recognise the spiritual dimension of any being. This is linked to the ability to mourn. We will write more about this further down (see transformation). The heart chakra is located in the middle of the sternum, in the middle of the chest, slightly higher than the physical heart.

Bob: "We have (placed) the four words (with this triangle). The three outer words in the triangle: peace-understanding-love. These are the three words that you need to have a relationship to, in directing energy to another person. You have to have peace in yourself. You have to have an increasing understanding of you and your connection with the other person. And you have got to have love in what you are doing. The word love, a very much misused word, but it is a word which has an exact meaning. But it's only seen when it is expressed. Right in the center where we have all of this combination of the two energies I am speaking about, prana and spiritual or higher consciousness energy, we placed the word joy. If you are working with other people and you don't have joy in what you are doing, you should stop working. Because you can't work with other people in compassion, if you don't have joy in what you are doing. Joy is the reality of expression."

Thyroid Chakra

Bob: "The heart chakra movement is showing up different from the thyroid-movement but when we come to a combination, then of course the whole aspect of healing is bringing the energies of both chakras into a formation, so that they can be used, not as separate chakras, but as two chakras reflecting two different states of vibration that in the - let us call it - penetration become one." He also repeated often that love (as a result of the transformation process) does not exist ....unless expressed. This again underlines the importance of the co-operation between heart chakra and thyroid, which is the chakra of expression. We find the thyroid

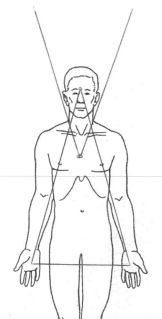

chakra just beneath the Adam's apple with men and in the lower part of the neck, in front.

The opposite of expression is suppression. Non-expression pushes what we don't express towards the bottom area of the body, around the pelvic area and the thighs, and this can then be seen as a blue colour in the aura - the blue of the thyroid again. The unexpressed themes remain in our subconscious until we bring them up to the surface again through the transformation work.

All the energy of the four lower chakras has to pass through the thyroid chakra in order to reach the pineal. All inspirational energy alsol has to move through the heart and the thyroid chakra. We have two lines of inspiration that form a V, coming through the collar bone points and reaching directly into the heart chakra (see tanka p. 79). This female triangle is the necessary counterpart in the transformation process, where the male triangle ▲ represents the energy coming from the bottom of the body. The hands have their natural connection to action, grasping and expression. The two triangles overlap, leaving the thyroid chakra in their middle, thus stressing once more the importance of this chakra in all transformation and inspiration.

Pineal Chakra

This chakra is linked to the centre of the head where the pineal and the pituitary glands are next to each other. The pituitary controls the endocrine gland system, while the pineal gland controls all the chakras. The pineal chakra extension on the forehead is found just where the eyebrows would meet.

The pineal chakra brings clairvoyance, the faculty to see clearly in our life, to see the direction to take, to perceive the sense of our life. Bob: "This sense cannot have an egotistic aim or self-gratification, but can only be linked to sharing and blend, an activity that is beneficial for everybody." All our potential as human beings seems to be contained in this chakra. In order to free this potential, its energy needs to come from the lower chakras. That energy has got to find its balance with the hara and be expressed through the qualities of the heart: compassion and joy. In the Bible Jesus says: "When your eye will be one, your body will be filled with light, but if you eye is not one it will be filled with darkness."

Crown Chakra

You cannot develop the crown chakra directly. Bob: "The crown will only operate in a balance, when other chakras of themselves are in a balance. ...the only way that can operate, that if the soul, your soul is to grow, it can only grow by having itself express through you physically. When that soul is expressed through you physically then that expression is creating experience. That experience has got to move through the different chakras to the crown-chakra and from the crown-chakra we have this relationship to the ID-point, which some people call the soul ..." The crown chakra is found in a horizontal position situated just above the hair on the top of the head. It is linked to all the other chakras but more so to the heart chakra. Its inner circulation has got 12 sections like the heart chakra and its outer circulation is made of 960 sections.

Each link between two chakras forms a particular theme. Let us take as an example the three following pairs:

> Root – thyroid, the theme of expression
> Hara – pineal, the theme of control
> Solar plexus – crown, the theme of blend and balance

Seven Gates to Heaven

Each of the seven major chakras is in itself a teaching, opening a gate to heaven:

- Root chakra – I surrender to and accept myself; I feel, love and accept my body with all its parts (see meditation on the body)
- Hara – peace of body and mind; I am aware of my breath
- Solar Plexus – I practice love and understanding

- Heart – I am joy and compassion
- Thyroid chakra – my inner becomes the outer and vice versa
- Third eye – when the two become one (eyes, male – female)
- Crown chakra – I am celebrating life in the present

(see my album 'Seven Gates to Heaven')

21 secondary chakras

the pairs :   feet, knees, pubic bone, eyes, ears, chest, hands, spleen

single points : 1st depression point, 2nd depression pt., stomach, liver, thymus

Before describing the secondary chakras and the other energy points that we use, I would like to remind you of the impermanence and interdependence of all things. I advise you to not simply take this list of points and the definitions given here and think that this corresponds exactly to reality. This is not the case. Bob's words come to my mind when I presented him with a glossary of these points and energy structures that I had put together: "This is very good, but taken out of context." It is like attempting to define a pond or an oak and the verbal descriptions will not match the reality of the pond or the oak. Each energy point is part of a context through which we can get a glimpse of our state of health/consciousness. If we do not have the means to observe the context, the definitions of these points alone will be of little help. The secondary chakras and other energy points give us paths of research, paths to walk down – with open eyes and hearts.

These points are located on the etheric. In my diagram I place or draw them on the physical body in order to show their precise location and to be able to describe them here in this book. This contributes to a precision of work, as much when done on ourselves as when working on others in a healing session. We suggest that you work with these points and thus gain understanding and experience about them before using them on others.

The secondary chakras distribute the energy that comes from the major chakras. Each secondary chakra has therefore got a link with one or possibly more major chakras that are located near it.

Secondary chakras in pairs

Feet – These correspond to the Solar Plexus area in Reflexology. They are found in the middle of the sole of the foot at the front of the arch and are linked to the root chakra and to all zones of our body through the positive psychic stream. They play a predominant role in our contact to the earth, to daily life, to our sense of direction and to the decisions we take as well as to our sense of security and success.

Grounding exercise using these feet points: Start at hara – moving slowly on the skin surface down the right leg to the secondary chakra underneath the right foot – move over through the air to the left foot point – move up the left leg on skin surface to the hara. Repeat slowly for ten minutes. During this time you should not be doing more than two to three complete circulations.

Knee points – They are situated in the knee and are also linked to the root chakra, to sexuality, shocks, and with events of early childhood. The two energy points linked with these secondary chakras are found on the negative stream on the inside of the knee on the tendon.

It can be very helpful to work on the knees in the polarity position, using the palm of your right hand on the left knee and the left hand on the right knee, either in treatment or on yourself. 2-3 minutes

Pubic bone points – they are situated on top of the pubic bone about two cm on each side of the middle. They are part of the negative steams and have a connection to the hara and the root chakra. They are linked to the ovulation-menstruation cycles of the female and to sexual expression. With women they are important during the pre-menstruation and emotional phase. They are also strongly linked to the thyroid chakra, to blend, openness of mind, and to a movement out. In those points there are movements of energy going out and in.

These are two excellent points to improve the contact to the lower body. You can work on them using **a triangle exercise** from the reflector point or from the navel, both in treating another person or on yourself. Move from starting point down to the left pubic bone point, pause, move across to the right point, pause again then move back up to the starting point. 3-5 minutes

Eyes – These secondary chakras are behind the eyes. The eyes have a strong link to the solar plexus. The left eye is linked to the pituitary gland, the right eye to the pineal gland and the pineal chakra. The pineal gland controls the lower five chakras.

Ears – the two chakras are found beneath the ears on the jaw structure. These points are part of the positive streams and distribute energy that is coming from the thyroid chakra. They will register states of stress and can be used to regulate arterial tension.

Chest – These two points are located above the nipples slightly to the centre. They are of course linked to the theme of the heart chakra and to the expression or non-expression of love. They are very active during breast feeding and are part of the female movement of energy going out in the chest area. With men this movement is opposite. These points would be limited in their action if a person is holding on to grief.

Hands – found in the middle of the palm of the hand. They are polarity points that carry the energy of the heart and are linked to our way of expressing. These points are in fact linked to all the major chakras and play an important role in the transformation of energy towards the third eye. These secondary chakras are part of the negative arm streams. When someone is working with massage or healing through the hands, these secondary chakras grow and their energy will then cover the whole surface of the hand. These points have a great influence on our behaviour, our control and our compassion, all we do towards others. Hands are so important in all our activities.

Triangle Exercise using hands and pineal : Move from the pineal down to the right hand, drawing the lines on the skin surface across in the air to the left hand and up again to the pineal. This can help us to connect with the deeper aspects behind our actions and thus to bring a better feeling and intuitive contact into what we are doing with our hands.

Spleen points – There are two secondary chakras next to each other on the seventh rib near the spleen. This has sometimes misled people to think that the spleen is a major chakra. According to our definition, this is not the case, because it cannot be developed. The upper secondary chakra at the spleen absorbs prana energy (see further down), whilst the lower secondary chakra at the spleen of the points distributes that energy to some major chakras. The hara chakra receives this energy via the root and the pineal chakra receives it through the thyroid chakra. The spleen points are part of the liver stream.

Single secondary chakras

1st depression point – This point is situated at the lower end of the sternum. It may be painful when you exert pressure on it. Any depression starts at the bottom of the lungs and spreads out towards the head and will eventually cover the whole head area, if it is not dealt with. In my understanding all states of depression originate in a lack of contact with spirituality and with our essence. This can be felt as a despair of being unable to reach higher consciousness and to express it. The energy at the chest level is thus pressed down, depressed and cannot find the necessary expansion. Grounding is certainly one vital aspect that is helpful in dealing with depression.

The first depression point is part of the negative arm stream and linked to the four levels of the etheric. This point can be affected by the impact that external authorities have had upon us, especially when this is in the way of us finding our own authority. In order to contact our own essence it is necessary to work with this depression point. If there is a limitation in the transformation of energy from the solar plexus to the heart, you would see it at this point. When we have transformed its restrictions this point is also linked to joy and to the heart.

2nd depression point – situated above the thymus gland and its secondary chakra, at the upper end of the sternum where the collar bones meet. There is a direct link from that point to the essence stream in the spine. A lack of contact with our essence contributes to depression. This point is part of the negative arm stream.

Thymus point – This endocrine gland which plays an important part in the body's immune system and is naturally active during childhood and up to puberty. Young children are more vulnerable to the emotions of other people around them because their thymus gland is still large and this is linked to the influx of spiritual energy. When this is interrupted the gland tends to shrink. The thymus can be reactivated and revitalised through spiritual development, in which case it can hurt for a certain time.

Stomach point – linked to digestion, the stomach and the transversal part of the colon. You can find it about three fingers above the navel lightly towards the left. It is a point where energy can be retained linking to the experiences of birth and early childhood. It can hold on to the memories of shocks and emotions from other people. In its freed state there is a movement of energy in two directions: going in and out. Shocks in early childhood can affect the outward moving energy of this point and may lead to digestive problems later on. During a release through healing this point can recover more freedom.

Daniel Perret – The Science of Spiritual Healing

Liver point – found on the 7th rib in a direct line below the nipple. It gives us precious information on our emotional and physical health. It is part of the Liver stream.

Energy points, 21 secondary chakras and 8 psychic streams

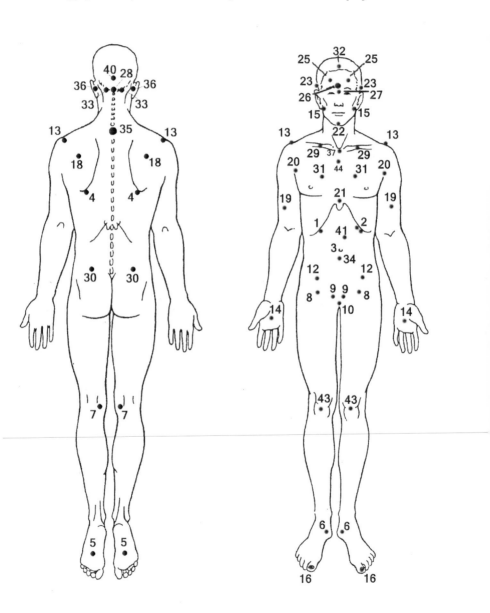

Daniel Perret – The Science of Spiritual Healing

1   liver point *
2   spleen * *
3   navel
4   shoulder blade pts.
5   soles of feet *
6   inner ankle points
7   knee pts.
8   groin pts.
9   pubic bone pts.*
10 G-spot
11 perineum pt. ¤
12 hip polarity pts.
13 shoulder polarity pts.
14 palm of hands *
15 under ear pts. *
16 tip of big toe
17 outer ankle points ¤
18 mid-shoulder blade pts
19 fever points
20 arm pit points
21 1st depression pt *

    * = secondary chakra
    ¤ = not shown here

22 3rd depression pt
23 above ear points
24 centre of head ¤
25 memory or lobe pts
26 pineal extension pt
27 point of silence
28 medulla
29 collar bone points
30 thrust points
31 breast points *
32 reflector point
33 side medulla points
34 heat point
35 waste energy position
36 behind ear points ¤
37 2nd depression pt.*
38 behind front teeth ¤
39 soft/hard pallet pt. ¤
40 blend point, 4 fingers
    above 28
41 near stomach pt. *
42 eyes *
43 knees *
44 thymus *

Positive streams : 5 - 17 - 12 - 4 - 18 - 13 - 26 - 33 - 36 - 23 - 15
Negative streams : 6 - 7 - 9 - thyroid Chakra - 39 - 38 - 26
Liver steam :   2 - 3 - 1 - 4 - 4 - 2
neg. arm stream :   34 - 37 - 20 - 19 - 14 - major finger
pos. arm stream :   28 - 35 - 13 - fingertips
essence stream :   inside spine

43 other energy points 'on' the body

The pairs: hip bone points, shoulder points, thrust points, shoulder blade points, mid-shoulder blade points, collar bone points, above ear points, behind the ear points, memory points, side medulla points, arm pit points, inner ankle points, outer ankle points, fever points, groin points, knee points

Single points: reflector point, blend point, medulla, point of silence, 3rd depression point, soft pallet, behind front teeth, coccyx, perineum / G spot, waste energy position, heat point, navel

The pairs

Hip bone points – You find the hip bone points on the upper edge of the pelvis, where it sticks out in front of the body. The exact location is about two cm below the part sticking out, just where the tendons of the legs start. These are important polarity points and give access to the pelvic area. They accumulate energy before expression, more on the left with the male, and more on the right point with the female. These points reflect both lower and upper astral states of consciousness (expansion, stability of thoughts & control of emotions). They can be used to help establish a better control when the solar plexus is too open and being affected by other people's emotions. These points are related to the storage of energy and can also be used to help restore a balance of energy where there has been a shock situation.

Two polarity exercises

These two exercises give us a strong means to balance our two sides.

a) draw a line on skin surface starting on the left hip bone point, move up to the left shoulder point, move across the collar bone points to the right shoulder, then down to the right hip bone point and across again to the left hip bone point.

b) Draw a line again on skin surface starting at the left hip bone point,

move across to the right shoulder point, from there across the collar bones to the left shoulder point, then down across to the right hip bone point and over to the left hip bone point. The lines cross at the solar plexus. Excess tension in the solar plexus tends to be evacuated along those lines towards one of the four points, often creating thus an unbalance.

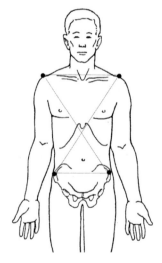

Shoulder points – The points can be found at the end of the collar bone points just behind their end on the flat part of the bone structure. They can hurt when pressed with a finger. They are important polarity points. A multitude of energy lines move through them: the rim of the mental aura, the positive arm streams, the positive body streams, the X cross through the solar plexus we have just mentioned. Tensions belonging to the solar plexus can sometimes be found in one of them.

The right shoulder point can hold on to strong emotions. The left shoulder point is an important entry point for spiritual energy moving in towards the heart along the rim of the mental aura. All infiltration of emotions slows down mental activity. We can easily see with these points how the thought energy can provoke a physical reaction through the movements of the arms.

Thrust points – these points draw their energy from the etheric storage in the pelvic area. When you want to push someone forward, for example a child, you would push them exactly there above the sacrum. The points can be found on the upper edge of the pelvic bone structure at the back. Depending on the anatomy you can feel them easily because the skin is directly on the bone, creating a small hollow. These points are linked to the activity of the lower torso: emotional and postural balance, seminal glands, prostate, ovaries, ovulation cycle, and expansion of consciousness. These thrust points take part in a movement of energy that goes up on the side of the spine, if this movement is not hindered by blockages (see the six blockage zones on the spine).

Shoulder blade points – the points sit on the 7th rib just underneath the corner of the shoulder blades. The liver stream and the positive stream cross here. Since these points are situated on the back, they are both strength positions.

Mid-shoulder blade-points – affected by the acidity-alkaline balance of the body

Daniel Perret – The Science of Spiritual Healing

Collar bone points – They are found about 2/5th from the inner part of the collar bone in a line with the side of the neck. They are linked to events around birth and early childhood. I have the impression that they have a strong link to spirituality, already in early childhood and also to how adults may have influenced us as children on the subject. They are the entry point of the inspiration lines.

Above ear points – approximately two cm above the ears, where the belief streams come out of the head. These points are thus linked to the centre of the head and the two hemispheres of the brain. They are linked to physical and mental stress.

Behind ear points or **awareness points** – are found just above the middle of the back of the ear where you can feel a little indenture in the bone structure. Linked to ear problems (wax, inflammation, inner ear), linked to the pituitary gland, blend, better judgment about one's life, conscious impulses, awareness in hearing, sensitivity, objective feelings, feeling of being linked to all that is. Certain kind of tinnitus problems can be linked to a malfunctioning of this point. Help to get a better blend, a harmonisation, aware of impulses, what I want to 'hear' and respond to, attraction, tuning in, objective feeling.

Memory points – three fingers above the middle of the eyebrows. They connect to our memory process and link any part of the body with memorized experiences. They are part of an etheric flow that includes the thrust points and the side medulla points.

Side medulla points – we find them on the lower edge of the skull at the back, on both sides of the medulla, where the two large muscles (capitis) that follow the spine are fixed to the skull. These points can often hold onto tension which has its origin in the lower part of the body. These two muscles come all the way up from the thrust points.

Arm pit points – They are part of the negative arm stream and can be found in the middle of the edge of the biceps in front of the arm pit and are linked to the heart energy.

Fever points – These points are part of the negative arm streams and are on the biceps, two fifth down the upper arm. Through the negative stream these points are linked to the heat point and to the bottom of the body. Most fever conditions have their origin in the bottom of the body, where there is a strong link between the etheric and the water area of the body. Pressure on these points can relieve some states of fever as well as sleepiness.

Outer ankle points – These points are on the positive streams. We find them in the middle of a line between the tibia and the edge of the heel. The four ankle points are very efficient in treating digestive problems linked to the solar plexus. They can help to temporarily remove energy from the solar plexus area when we wish to work there with healing.

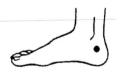

Inner ankle points – They are on the negative streams. They are situated in the middle of a line between the tibia and the edge of the heel.

Groin points – to be found in the middle of the groin, they are linked to the lymph system. The left point is therefore very active. Both points are linked to sexuality and the evacuation of problems related to the sacrum. They take part in the link between the pubic bone points and the hip points, thus linking the positive and the negative streams.

Knee points – These points are on the negative streams and are found on the tendon inside the knee.

The single points
Heat point – s situated two fingers width beneath the navel and is linked to sexuality and elimination. This point produces heat in two ways: the bottom of the body is creating heat in the preliminary phases of sexual activity and produces an effect on the right perineum point with males. This movement generates a flux of blood into the penis. When the heat point is not taking part in sexual activity it moves the energy towards the upper part of the body and can sometimes be felt as an overall warmth in the body.

Navel – connects to vitality, life force, movement and is linked to all the parts of the body. The navel links to birth, pre-birth conditions and to the months after birth as well as to many aspects connected with our mothers and with intimate relationships. It can also retain the emotional impacts of separations. The impact of shock situations affects the navel area and can inhibit our expression and the control over our energy. An energy blockage here can sometimes be felt as a circle around the navel, which we can feel e.g. when we do the liver stream, moving to and from the navel on skin surface. Once freed the energy around the navel can open out into a feeling of being connected with everything.

Reflector point – Is located a little above the hair line at the front, on top of the head on the centre line, eight fingers above where the eyebrows would meet. Working with this point will deepen an opening towards higher consciousness through the draw in of light to the bottom of the body. It increases our means to control emotions. Difficulties in contacting it could therefore come from blockages in the bottom of the body.

Blend point – is situated four fingers above the medulla where the little finger is when you place the index finger in the medulla. It is linked to all levels of consciousness and to the blend of thought, expression and to the metabolism balance in the body. 'Blend' is the natural coming together of several structures and all the energy levels are connected here. The blend point reflects harmony within ourself and working with it can thus aid this process. The blend point is linked to the cerebellum **(floccunodular lobe), and** is also known as the silver chord. During the death process our energy is drawn to this point and it is from here that our consciousness leaves the body.

Medulla – is situated in the groove in the neck at the bottom of the skull. The point is linked to the expansion of consciousness. We can observe an expansive movement of energy there when someone expresses freely, drawing upon their quality energy in a discussion. Emotional blockages, linked to having been affected by an authority or restricted in our expression can accumulate here.

Waste energy position – Waste energy is created by a lack of control over the energy in the lower part of the body. It accumulates in this position on the upper back in layers of energy that are drawn there at different periods. Smaller or larger amounts of energy can accumulate here and can feel like a cushion, situated around the second dorsal vertebrae, just above the heart chakra energy. Once in a while it is advisable to have this stagnant energy worked on and thus put back into circulation to avoid it building up and causing back pain.

Coccyx – is situated at the very base of the spine. Energy blockage in this area would link to early childhood, the balance or lack of balance in relationships, resistance, fear of the opposite sex, frustration that also shows at the 3rd lumber vertebrae.

G spot – The Gräfenberg point is found in the inside of the vagina at the front and was discovered by a German medical doctor in the seventies. It has a slightly magnetic quality which draws the attention there. It is a very powerful point for improving contact to the genital organs and to the whole water area of the body. The G spot is very important in the understanding of female sexuality. For a long time it was neglected by male teaching traditions (mostly from India) which only worked with the perineum point with men. This point helps to harmonise the male and female energies in females and links to spirituality.

Perineum point – located between the anus and genitals in the male. It has sometimes been described as the root chakra. In our definition it is not a major chakra since it cannot be developed. The perineum point affects the prostate. Like the G spot it is a point of fusion of the hara and the root chakra energy. The equivalent point with females is the G spot and has a similar function.

3rd Depression point – The point is in the middle of the chin. It is related to stress and is affected when a person becomes bipolar or manic-depressive.

Point of silence – this point is found on the bridge of the nose and is linked to the pituitary gland. Any connection to silence in meditation links to this point, whether consciously or not. We can learn to neutralise disturbing noises by drawing them into this point, consciously and slowly and thus disconnect from the emotional content.

Point on the soft pallet of the mouth – where the soft pallet meets the hard pallet, this point is on the negative stream.

Point behind front teeth – on the negative stream
The point behind the two front teeth at the top and the point going into the soft pallet of the mouth are two points that reflect the energy from the combined movement between the root and the hara.

6 blockage zones on the spine
- 3rd cervical, beginning point for certain migraines, worrying
- Waste energy position, 2nd dorsal
- Point of impact of the solar plexus, 5th – 7th dorsal
- 3rd lumbar vertebrae, where the male and female energy meets, suppression linked to sexuality, constipation and diarrhoea
- Zone between sacrum and lumber vertebrae
- Coccyx

The eight psychic streams
These streams are channels along which energy runs. They link the etheric to the physical. Each stream has its specific function. The energy in the streams runs two ways, as all energy movement does. These steams have two end points

with neither being the beginning or the end as such. We must always work with a positive and a negative stream when we want to produce an effect. It is similar with electricity. Bob: "The psychic streams are like cables that run horizontally along the etheric. They need to be in a balanced state so that the etheric can do its job as a store of energy, allowing that energy to penetrate into the physical level." "The psychic streams are in the body to allow energy activity to be moved from one area to another area. This energy activity brings us into other states of consciousness as reflected through different chakras, that relates to what we call higher consciousness or spiritual awareness."

It takes at least a year of personal exploration with these streams to establish a good connection: three months for the liver stream, three for the positive and negative streams, 2-3 months for the arm streams and three months for the essence stream. You need this amount of time to work with them yourself and to plan this length of time when you teach it. If you don't work with these streams and experience them yourself you will not have the means to answer questions and to explain what happens with other people. Together with the grounding exercises these eight streams form an initiation in itself.

All these streams can be worked on by following their lines and points on the skin surface, very slowly, pausing at each point, taking at least a 20 minute period for each stream. With the exception of the liver stream and the spine stream one always combines a negative and a positive stream when working with them. The two arm streams connect in various ways, for example at the fingertips. The body streams again can be connected in various ways. An obvious place is the pineal chakra, where the two positive and two negative body streams meet.

Negative arm streams

Heat point – 2nd depression point (where it divides into two) – collar bone points – under arm pit points – fever points – (continuing on the inside of the arm) – secondary chakras of the hands – tip of the major finger

This stream collects energy in the bottom of the body when it is ready to be moved to the heart and to the hands, passing through the solar plexus and the heart area. This psychic stream is extremely beneficial for therapists who use their hands in their treatments. When it functions correctly we may feel the energy buzzing in our hands. On its way this stream works on obstacles that inhibit the energy that comes into our hands. The hands have an important role of in the whole transformation of energy as well as in expression and inspiration. In working with healing or massage the secondary chakras in the hands will enlarge and eventually cover the entire hand.

Positive arm stream

Blend point – waste energy position (where the stream divides into two) - shoulder points – (follow the exterior of the arm) – fingertips.

This positive arm stream moves through our back and strength area. This stream starts to function automatically when the negative arm streams work properly.

Positive body stream   (left and right)

Points on Positive Stream: Secondary chakra underneath the foot – exterior ankle point – hip bone point – shoulder blade point – mid shoulder blade point – shoulder points – pineal chakra (the two streams meet here and divide again and continue on both sides of the centre line on top of the head) – side medulla points – awareness points behind ears – above ear points – secondary chakras beneath the ears

When the positive streams don't function properly, the pineal chakra is affected and we need too much sleep. The right stream is naturally stronger than the left. There are much less emotional problems held in the positive body streams. Energy blockages here mostly come from emotional contacts with accidents and muscle damage while moving arms, legs and body.

Negative body stream (left and right)
Points on Negative Stream: Interior ankle point – knee point – pubic bone point – up on each side of the middle line of the body – thyroid chakra (where both streams meet) – point at the soft pallet – behind top front teeth – pineal chakra

When a negative stream does not work correctly the pineal chakra is affected and we may suffer from insomnia. The left stream is naturally stronger than the right because of the lymph vein that runs up on the left side of the torso. The predominant restriction aspects are found in these negative streams (emotional hold, resistance, escape mechanisms).

Liver stream
This stream follows the 7th rib except at the navel: spleen – navel – liver point – right shoulder blade point – left shoulder blade point – spleen.

The liver stream is the only horizontal stream in the body and thus all the other vertical streams pass through it. This stream is activated at our birth and working with it brings us into a deep feeling contact with ourselves. Working with the liver stream is excellent for digestive problems and helps to re-establish the contact with the lower part of the body partly through freeing the diaphragm. The liver stream can hold on to suppression states related to inadequate response or non- expression of emotions that may have their origin in childhood. Working between the reflector point and points on the liver stream can help to release this. This stream **should not be used** on or by pregnant women. It is also not advisable to use the liver stream at the same time as using one of the seven vertical streams as these could get overloaded. The distribution of energy into the vertical streams happens naturally over time after having worked with the liver stream. (see also Solar Plexus chakra)

Essence stream inside the spine
This stream links to our inner core and to the ID point and controls all the other streams as it is directly linked with them. The arm streams for instance, create that link at the waste energy position and at the 2nd depression point. The essence stream runs inside the spine from the heat point up to the centre of the head.

Drawing to the end of this chapter I would like to remind you that these structures are not the beginning and end of everything. Our aim in teaching the use of these points and streams is to bring precision which helps you to come into a depth of feeling with yourself. It is this depth of feeling that allows you to progress the connection to your essence level which lies beyond even those invisible structures.

Energy points and structures outside the physical body
The energy fields are by definition non-physical and are outside our physical body, except for the etheric that is partly inside the body. Up until now we have only described points

that we have a reference point for on the physical body which helps us to locate them precisely. I will now describe a number of structures outside the physical body which are also part of our energy make-up. (There are also impermanent structures in our energy field which are blockages created by problems).

Belief streams – In my understanding these streams form the first manifestation of our vertical current. After this the vertical current finds another level of manifestation at each chakra through its particular expression. The belief streams start in the centre of the head, a very important area, between the pituitary and the pineal gland. They come out from the head at the points above the ears and can extend very far out, further out than the spiritual part of the aura. You can quite easily detect them with your hands. The belief streams are the home of our beliefs, the thought structures that form the bases of our thinking and our actions. Any work with affirmations will affect these streams. We usually form our primary beliefs during childhood and adolescence in that we take over the beliefs of parents and authorities. Ideally our own reflection and life experience will allow us to develop our own beliefs.

Focus position – The focus position has the shape of a pizza and is situated just above the rim of the mental aura around the vertical stream. It is situated in the emotional aura. It is good to remember this, because when we try to contact our ID point or our divine consciousness we may meet emotions and this often seems to happen precisely at the focus position. Our doubts about the divine, about spirituality and higher consciousness may get in the way. The centre of the focus position is relatively free of emotions, whereas emotions tend to accumulate near to the edges and, it is these areas that normally attract our attention. The energy of the focus position is composed of different energy activities: it reflects the energy of each chakra, of your thoughts, emotions, spirituality and your beliefs. When there is a limitation in any of those areas, the focus position cannot expand.

Inspiration lines – These lines come from beyond our spiritual aura in a V shape or female triangle and meet, passing through the collar bone points that reach the heart chakra. We will describe them later in the paragraph on transformation. They are depicted in a Tibetan thangka of the medicine Buddha Sakyamuni. (see drawing above, on page 79)

Etheric eyes – also called the sensing points of the etheric. They are found in the etheric above the head. I show them in the drawing on page 25 positioned on the slightly higher line above the head, on each side of the centre stream. If a person has developed their intuitive perception, their etheric will have expanded and the etheric eyes will thus be higher up in the etheric .We can say that our sixth sense is situated there. In fact all our senses are etheric senses.

Cross of the heart – This is the only other energy cross in our make up after the belief streams. We might want to think about that.

Emanations of the chakras – Each chakra has movements of energy going in and out, at the front and at the back. These differ from chakra to chakra. The drawing on page 26 shows that the impact point on the spine is higher than the opening of the chakra at the front where it is located just above the skin surface. This upward movement follows a similar path as the nervous system.

Happiness point – This point is situated in front of the body in the spiritual part of the aura at the level of the navel / solar plexus. When we have worked through energy blockages at the level of the navel we can be drawn to the happiness point that connects us to a feeling of at-one-ment. Contact with this point can help to takes us beyond worries.

Points outside the feet – In one of our basic exercises we work with a triangle from the ID point. First we make contact with the ID point then we draw a line in the aura structure, down the right side of the body about 10-20 cm from the skin, to reach a point outside the right foot. We take some time to feel this point, before continuing. We then move the line across, passing underneath the feet to reach a point outside the left foot. We take some time to feel this point, before continuing. From there we move back up to the ID point, again keeping some distance away from the body. Draw the lines with closed eyes, slowly and feel what is happening as you move along. Feel any difference between left and right, beginning, middle and end of a side of the triangle.

The two feet points are realities and each can tell us a story about our contact with the ground, about the way we take steps in life (right foot) and about how grounded our point of view is (left foot). The interpretation mainly depends on the situation of the person. Some general observations: right side = masculine and expression side, left side = feminine, feelings, intuition, emotions; ID point = our contact with our soul, our spirituality; obstacles along the lines can be linked to the body zone or chakra on the same level.

Incoming and outgoing energy at points – Each energy point has one or several spirals of energy moving into it from the outside and one or more lines that move away from it.

Overall etheric circulation – The etheric has two overall movements of energy that connect head and feet and all the zones in between, front and back. They distribute energy. One movement comes up the front on our left side, pivots over the left belief stream and moves down the back to the underneath the feet, pivots there and moves up again. On the right side the stream comes up the back and down the front. This movement of energy gives the general direction to all the energy movements at the front and at the back (circulation of chakra, of torso energy, etc.).

A good way to end a healing treatment is by doing an etheric massage along those streams. This helps to bring energy that has been freed up during the healing session back into its natural circulation. You would move your hands in the etheric several times up one side and down the other, 'brushing' the energy following the direction of the streams.

When we empty ourselves
Of all that attaches us to Creation
And we liberate ourselves from this for the love of the Divine
Then this very same Divine will fill us with itself.

Teresa of Avila

To love means to die a little each day.

If we want our heart to be totally ready,
It must rest upon absolute emptiness.

Master Eckhardt

The Process - the adventure

The concrete experience of the spiritual

In our western societies we need to deal with a major obstacle. Anything that has got to do with the invisible may not only put our sciences in an uncomfortable position but also confronts us with our religious heritage. We may think that we are atheists or have turned our backs on the church a long time ago, but our history, our collective culture and usually our personal and family culture is permeated with the theme of religion and the Christian church. I am convinced this is the same for other continents and religions.

When we begin to contact our ID point, at arm's length above our heads, we may not feel anything and find ourselves confronted with doubts or critical judgments. Leaving the known reference point of our physical body we can feel as if we are at sea. For newcomers it can be helpful, at this point, to suspend judgement and take time to experiment with sensing and feeling energy in order to build up personal experience and thus gradually develop trust in a new dimension. This can lead to a fundamental change of belief about the nature of reality.

I spent ten months in a beautiful Anthroposophical centre south of Stockholm at the beginning of the eighties. I was lucky to see with what creativity and devotion the researchers at a Biodynamic centre were working on improving seeds. They were inspired by the inestimable work of Rudolf Steiner who lived at the beginning of the 20th century. As I was already studying the human energy fields with Bob Moore, I practised sensing energy around plants, huge anthills and trees. In the beginning, I was convinced that I could not sense anything invisible with my hands. When I succeeded I tried to show this to the researchers – who were used to drawing energy fields around a plant as Steiner had taught them. I was astonished when I realised that feeling and observing energy fields with their own hands did not interest them at all. Apparently Steiner had not told them how to sense energy with the hands. There is no doubt that he had exceptional clairvoyant faculties. I have no idea whether these researchers changed their way of thinking later on. I share this just to illustrate how much our beliefs can limit us.

As we begin to explore spiritual healing we will be confronted with our limiting beliefs and sometimes with strong emotions. We need to deal with them before we can experience spirituality in a tangible way. It is not that the spiritual or the invisible is inaccessible or secret - it is we who have excluded ourselves from these dimensions. Transforming emotions opens up the way of the heart, the way of feelings. Without a feeling connection we cannot explore the invisible, the spiritual. (see my book 'The concrete experience of Spirituality', BOD publications, 2011)

Key beliefs, faith and trust

In all serious exploration of an object the researcher will be questioning the system of beliefs he operates within and this is the same when we explore spiritual healing. During childhood we construct the bases of our thinking from values taken over from parents, school teachers, moral and religious authorities. Later on we need to question our basic beliefs and then formulate our own values as some of our beliefs can be creating limitations. Faith makes up the part of our belief system that is concerned with the spiritual, universal, mystical, mythological and religious dimensions, depending on our vocabulary. These beliefs, including atheist or nihilist convictions are held in our belief streams. We must explore following question: if our personal beliefs are not rooted in other people's beliefs, what are they actually based on? Is it a deep feeling, an experience, the experience of our life or is it our accumulated emotions and deceptions?

We all have our ideas about life, death, the existence or not of life forms between lives, guardian angels, spiritual guides, the creation of the world, the use of prayer, respect of life, nature, animals, universal values, the meaning of life. Only when our faith is a personally defined one, can we come to trust in its reality and thus its application in our lives. Sailors in the olden days who set out to reach America oriented themselves by the stars, with tools and maps, and then trusted the initial decision they had taken. When the sky became cloudy they mostly knew that keeping to their direction was the only thing to do.

Bob: "...in belief there is a means to obtain a contact with a higher source. It doesn't matter whether your belief relates to Mohamed or to Christ or God or Universal Consciousness or whatever, if that belief has given you the means to open yourself, to be receptive to a higher state of consciousness, then you can use that higher state of consciousness because you have increased the activity of the energy flow through your whole being and that is what shows in your aura structure.. ....of course this is going to be more effective if you have reached a state of your consciousness in which you are not holding on to your blockages or whatever. "

Transformation

A major part of Bob's teaching was directed towards connecting to the spiritual quality of each chakra through a gradual process of transformation of its emotional content. Each chakra thus has got its own polarity. The qualities of the four lower chakras correspond to the manifestation or the original pure spirit: the root - feeling successful, the hara -calm and at peace, the solar plexus - feeling love and understanding and, for the heart- compassion and joy.

The emotional content of each chakra can be transformed through the intention and clarity of our minds. The Tibetans have known this capacity for hundreds of years and compare it to the gradual heating of a cold room by fire, or to a jar of cold water into which one pours hot water. The plasticity of the brain has been discovered fairly recently by neuroscience and confirms our capacity to change. Even at an advanced age the brain retains its' capacity to renew its' cells and to develop new connections, to improve and adapt its' functioning.

The transformation of our emotions towards their spiritual potential happens in two phases. During the first phase the contact with the lower part of the torso and the three lower chakras has to be improved, these energies have to be set in motion so as to free and move them towards the solar plexus , the fire area of the body. This is called the *transmutation* phase. Here the energies are *transformed* in a movement from the solar plexus to the heart chakra. This is the direction that psychotherapy of all kinds has undertaken since Sigmund Freud began his work in the early 20th century. The psycho-energetic approach of Bob Moore adds a new component: the notion of energy and spiritual qualities that allow us to progress beyond the trapped energy of traumas from childhood or later life. Bob's approach certainly involves working with trauma, but their ultimate transformation is brought about by replacing the emotional energy of the trauma with spiritual energy.

Transmutation of energy of the lower body

This first phase of the transformation process requires for a disciplined and continuous effort. We aim to bring into consciousness what has been hidden in the subconscious, our shadows: habits, traumas, emotions. This change is brought about through the control of the upper mental and the guidance of the spiritual. The astral has an intelligence that resists changes and it fights to maintain its hold over us. Suppressed emotion is held around the lower part of the torso and the thighs. We have an unconscious mechanism of pushing down emotions that we have not had the means to process. Stored around the lower part of the body they are far away from the head area and the thyroid chakra (expression versus suppression). There is a natural connection between the water area, the subconscious and the etheric (storage of subconscious memory). All personal experience that is not finding an expression either through thoughts, words or actions gets stored in the subconscious.

In order to deal with habits of suppression and the capacity of the astral to defend emotions, we need to employ efficient techniques such as the use of precise points (secondary chakras and other energy points.) We'll come back to this later. It is easier and more efficient to contact these points than to work exclusively with the major chakras alone, such as the *root, hara* and *solar plexus*. The contact with the root and the hara alone may remain vague and not concrete enough for many years. You can compare this work to a guided tour of a nuclear power station. You cannot completely grasp its way of functioning. It's only though working with these energy points, comparable to a detailed study and experience of the various 'subsystems' of the power station, that we can start building up our understanding. Neuroscience can only help us up to a point, because it only deals with the 'control room' of the power station. Neuroscientists observe little lamps as they light up and turn off and sometimes they seem to mistake them for the real elements of our mind and body.

The transformation process starts with getting a good and felt contact with a number of points. These points gradually enlarge, when worked on with our awareness. Whilst the initial contact with, for example, a pubic bone point can feel difficult or non existent at the beginning this will gradually improve. The next step is that of connecting a number of points and thus setting the energy in motion. The principle behind this is that

energy tends to go back to its source

as in an electric circuit, where the surplus of energy goes back to the electric power plant via the negative wire. Higher consciousness energy brings precision and a faster vibration to dissolve blockages. I believe there is another law that says

slow and blocked energy attracts faster energy

Or in other words it attracts attention. This faster energy eventually manages, through the principle of **resonance**, to accelerate the blocked, slow moving energy and thus helps it to get back into circulation. Another law governs the use of energy in this process:

Energy follows thought

Moving energy in the bottom of the body puts us in contact with the content of the subconscious. Improving the contact with these parts of our body makes suppressed emotions and memories accessible, allowing them to be worked with. I know of no other way to transform energy than to improve the contact to our body which is our radar of perception, in order to access the memories that are held there. We need perseverance and trust to work with such processes that may at times be intense and painful, but which lead to expansion and real liberation.

That is where the help of spiritual energy becomes necessary. Instead of turning around in vicious circles, the emotions we wake up are replaced by understanding, patience, self acceptance and above all with love. It is a two way process, a double movement: the upward movement from the bottom area of the body and the downward movement of spiritual energy, which replaces the emotions removed. Without this downward flow of spiritual energy the emotions would return to fill the void created by their dislodgment.

All phases of the transformation process require a disciplined effort and often a conscious change of our beliefs and habits. One needs, above all, to be clear about one's motivation and aim. This process is about regaining control of our energy, of our 'nuclear power station'.

Until we do this our emotions will continue to control us, and we will continue to be governed by habitual subconscious patterns. Transformation needs to be undertaken in a patient and balanced way - this is the art of development. Over the years Bob Moore taught a progressive series of precise meditations, practices and numerous well timed energy exercises, allowing this gradual change of consciousness to take place, without danger or forcing. The aim of the phase of transmutation is to move the energy from the bottom of the body up to the solar plexus.

Transformation between solar plexus and heart
The last phase consists of allowing the energy that has been moved up the body to be transformed through *fire* in the solar plexus. This is the ultimate transformation of matter towards light, love, understanding and finally into joy and compassion. This transformation leads to a state of more human warmth and light (truth, understanding and joy being linked to light).

This process includes gradually leaving behind our individual and collective fears. The solar plexus chakra has a strong link to the astral and it is also here that emotions from outside can enter our system, creating tension or even sudden stomach aches. Symbols in dreams of fire or burning or of lower life forms such as insects may indicate external atmospheres or events that have had an impact upon the solar plexus. An instinctive emotional reaction is often to withdraw and close off, whereas the best way to protect ourselves from emotions is to feel them but to keep expressing in our lives. Love and comprehension are the qualities that we develop when we transform fear – the themes of the solar plexus.

In a development process we can be confronted with the four collective fears: fear of death, mental and physical illness, fear of sexuality – a vast subject. The time we live in seems to be confronting us with these fears and particularly with the phase of transformation through fire (explosives, nuclear power, terrorism, suicide bombers, and all the explosions in action films).

The experience of transformation is an individual one and can take different forms. Take for instance 'mourning' for someone who left us, through death or separation. A true state of mourning is an active transformation. This is opposite to self-pity, which is a trap and a non-productive emotion, because it takes away control. You become a victim, mainly of an illusion. Both unresolved grief and self-pity are the emotions linked to the heart chakra, that you may experience in the upper chest area. This area is strongly linked to the thymus gland which is responsible for the production of white blood cells and is an important part of our immune system. If you don't mourn after a death or a separation you may become depressed and this could affect your health and cause illness.

I am developing this in order to illustrate that unreleased tears can affect the stomach and the solar plexus chakra. The stomach can temporarily contract. We remember: the solar plexus chakra is where emotions from outside penetrate into our system. Unresolved emotions from previous lives can still be affecting the solar plexus. They create a point of attraction, a weakness in the solar plexus that then attracts similar emotions. Such emotions could for instance arise from having been in a position of responsibility in another life and having taken decisions that created suffering. This could for example, be the memory structure underlying the present emotions that we need to mourn, understand and clear. Through working with the energy of the solar plexus and the heart we can be led to transform grief into compassion, love and understanding. These are the themes of the two chakras: solar plexus and heart. This may seem complicated at first but works within quite a simple logic. The themes of each of the chakras give us precious indications as to the way of transforming what is held in each chakra.

Concentrating on our personal action

If you want to prevent a gifted gardener from being happy and from living his potential, make him responsible for regulating the traffic of a large city.

This is quite a serious problem of our time. We have created mass media that confront us daily with suffering and catastrophes from all over the world. We are now confronted with numerous very urgent situations that seem to have reached a point of no return: health systems, climate change, economy, intensive agriculture and its pollution, old age pension systems, etc. Many of these difficult situations may create desperation and hopelessness in us, so that we may loose a sense of control, not knowing how to contribute, how to cope without getting cynical. It is urgent that we focus on what we can realistically contribute and then learn to use our full spiritual potential or inborn qualities as this is where we are strongest and most efficient. All dispersion diminishes our impact and makes less effective and more vulnerable to fears and worries. It is to a certain extent an illusion to feel responsible for the suffering and problems of the world and this diverts us from our own responsibility. It is much easier to disperse by being busy than to live our strength and concentrate on what we can really change.

Bob gave us this old saying:

> Grant me the courage to change what I can change
> The strength to accept what I cannot change
> And the Wisdom to know the difference

Contacting our soul, our purpose in life

In my previous books I have written about the seven rays and the spiritual qualities. In the spiritual part of our aura they are pastel (increasingly pastel with use) colors which are with us right from birth. We usually have one or two quality colors: *red, orange, yellow, green, blue, rose pink or violet*. According to Alice Bailey the seven rays bring us awareness, each ray corresponding to a set of definite qualities. This is the essence of what makes us human beings and the seven rays are at the very core of our approach:

Red	courage, will, power, self dependant, leadership
Orange	balance, harmony, rhythm, beauty
Yellow	tolerance, patience, logic, precision
Green	impartial, adaptable, instinctive, mental strength
Blue	intuition, love, wisdom, perception
Rose pink	devotion, loyalty, service to others, directness
Violet	truth, ritualism, activity, integration, vitality, dignity

If we take the word 'power', we can be powerful and controlled by our emotions and ego, feeling superior to others and imposing our will. We can also use power with compassion and love, and this form of power is linked with spiritual structures or higher consciousness. The inborn quality for example of the red ray is essentially a power of non-interference. With most of the above words we can distinguish between these two levels.

If you wish to discover which ray you are on and gain insight into your own qualities, you can contact each color, trying to appreciate each one and experience what that color represents for you on a feeling level. You can then meditate on each word, starting for instance with the red ray and the word courage. You will find that certain words mean more to you than others. Whilst progressing through the list you can gradually eliminate some words and start to narrow down which color or colors you feel connected to. This takes time. You need to feel the deeper sense of a word and how it affects you. Try first of all to use the word out loud a bit like a mantra can be helpful, then say it silently within.

Meditating on each ray reveals their differences and can sometimes throw light on what seems an apparent incompatibility, for instance between a person living on a red ray and another person expressing from the orange ray. The first is a born leader, the second is for instance an artist. There could also be a type of clash between a person on a green ray and a person on a blue or pink ray.

The person on the green ray can have a strong mental power that may fill a whole room when they are present, especially if they are not using that power from a feeling and spiritual level. Unless they have learned to use their own spiritual strength a person who has a blue or pink ray could perhaps easily feel squashed by the mental strength of the green ray.

At first sight these differences can help us understand the challenges that can come about with two people living together (parent – child, boss – subordinate, etc.). The difficulty would arise from the emotional level, when a person has not really understood the spiritual quality of their ray as we saw in the example with the word 'power'. Any challenging situation can be an encouragement to live up to and express one's own qualities. It takes strength and determination to bring one's qualities into an expression. This can be even more so for a person who is living their first life on a ray. In my understanding these qualities are part of a positive karmic capital we have accumulated during past lives. It seems that we explore and learn to express through one particular ray or a number of lives before moving onto another.

Your quality color will not change during this life, however it will become a more refined pastel when you are using and expressing it. When a person is not using their qualities and does not try to develop them, the color will remain dull and the outer part of the aura will not show much movement and will lack vibrancy.

The contact with our soul can sometimes be felt like the inner voice of conscience, through inner movements of energy that push you to say or do things or move you to tears when you see the picture of someone you seemingly don't know or of someone playing the piano next door. You can also become aware of persistent feelings concerning your work, a person or a place. It can also show itself as a deep feeling in the heart. These impulses have little to do with logic and often cannot be explained, they are just here. We have periods where this feeling level is more at the surface as for instance in childhood or adolescence. Our sense of meaning in life is built upon respecting and recognizing these messages that come from deep within.

'Personal' and spiritual development
Once we accept that we are energy, surrounded by vast fields of energy, then we realize that we are linked to all that is, the perception of our self as an isolated independent being can then be seen as a complete illusion. From that point on all development includes everybody and everything. There is no such thing anymore as strictly 'personal' development even though our main focus will be our own process.
I would like to include some of the preface Bob Moore wrote for my first book "Music – The Feeling Way':

"The process of personal development is essentially that of learning about oneself, which involves the relationship to energy within the physical body and energy external to the physical body. One can find that the energy fields react to the various circumstances in which one becomes involved in one's life.

As one would move beyond the curiosity stage, which perhaps many are finding in their initial attraction to the process of energy and personal development, one becomes confronted with questions such as: Why would one wish to pursue the whole art of development? What is my motivation in wishing to develop? What am I going to use this increased knowledge of energy for? How do I understand the purpose of my life, through the increased awareness obtained within development? These questions are often confronting.

To work with energy within one's own structure of personal development is of itself a serious business, because one is required to make decisions, which often mean changes in one's life. It is necessary that such changes take place, because one so often realises that the things that one is doing are not helpful in progressing one's life, or what one is reaching towards as a goal has become too materialistic. As progress is made, various thoughts come forward as to what change means and if indeed it is possible to make changes in one's everyday activity. Development, in relationship to understanding one's own life, is not going to be accomplished within a few months or indeed a few years. It's progressive state, which one finds oneself involved with, lasts for the remainder of one's physical existence. The various processes that one becomes involved with in development are often taking us away from such things as pride in establishing something as superiority or indeed taking us away from many of the emotions which have controlled our life structure. Emotions like anger perhaps or jealousy are things that hinder us from being able to appreciate a deeper relationship to ourselves and as a consequence sometimes mean that our connection to other people has become rather superficial.

Being increasingly aware of the feeling connection to ourselves and the depths that one can experience, particularly in contact with the heart, brings us into a humbleness, in which we can appreciate a more real or true balance between ourselves and other people. Within this process one often becomes aware of the need to express the feelings that we have about areas which are linked to the depth of our true nature. This is where one can find various aspects will show up with different people, realising that personal development is not something that is the same for each person. Its individual connection shows itself in the individual ways to register and to express outward. The attraction to the various structures that appeal to us to be expressed (like music, art, etc.), then become part of the whole process one finds within development through the use of energy. "

And during a course: "The use of these four ethers that we see in the etheric are not just in our etheric, they are also in the etheric around the world. This is why, when we look at the development of any one person, it can never be a singular development, it has got to relate to other people, to the universe."

Personal development can never have an egotistic aim. Bob: "Development is linked to an opening and a sharing with everybody. There is no place for superiority in development. Some may show some superiority when they have learned to do certain psychic things with energy, but this is not necessarily part of development. Development in its essence, consists in reaching inside ourselves a means to progress so that we can share with others as equals. It is this equality, this process of sharing, which allows us to grow."

Forces that hinder the healing work

Some time ago I was introduced to the books and work of Marko Pogacnik and I find his method of healing the earth and places in a landscape remarkable. He builds a wonderful bridge between personal and global development and I feel there is some similarity between our approaches. I will present some of his thoughts on how to avoid looking for an external enemy as they are full of common sense. Projections onto an external enemy gives them power, taking away our control and leaving us a victim of our own fears, projections and unbalance. I am sure Marko would agree with the following statement:

> We cannot heal ourselves without healing the planet. We cannot heal the planet without healing ourselves. All begins with the experience of harmony and peace in us.

When working with healing and re-establishing a lost balance in nature or within ourselves obstacles may arise and seem to want to hinder the work. The opposition of constructive and so-called negative forces is an illusion and an unproductive belief. These phenomena actually prove to be very useful for any healing process when we learn to see them as signs of unbalance and disharmony, of disrupting a natural and sane state. According to Marko Pogacnik (Healing the Heart of the Earth: Restoring the Subtle Levels of Life, 1999) we can distinguish between:

1. Spirits or astral entities that were forced to take on a destructive role because of the aggressive behaviours

of humans who mistreated the vital systems to which they belong

2. Forces that became influenced by and have copied negative projections that human beings have created on a massive scale on earth
3. Destructive forces that were created by humans who consciously have altered constructive forces for egotistical aims, often resulting in power struggles hidden from the public.
4. Forces that have become chaotic and negative after the destruction of their environment on a subtle level. Most of the time these processes are based on human emotions of fear and hate.

I have transposed this list to fit our work of spiritual healing of individuals:

1. Our shadow, which is part of our personality that we deny; mistreated spirits of ancestors or excluded members of a family, etc.
2. Negative projections stemming from the four collective fears of death, madness, illness and sexuality, fears of change and fears of vitality
3. Black magic or similar forces
4. Pollution through chemical substances, electromagnetic pollution, noise, etc.

Exercises

The psycho-energetic exercises help us to get a better contact with our physical body and possible non-productive energy held in the etheric. Some exercises are intended to be used for a two to six month period, in order to achieve what they are meant to do. However some of these exercises can be re-used when one feels the need to do so - exercises for grounding, centring, the psychic streams, and especially the liver stream. The triangle exercises and the circulation using the four polarity points are other exercises that we have presented in this book can also be reused.

Grounding exercise
Stand with the feet apart, one foot slightly forward. Put all our weight and attention on the front foot whilst inhaling – then hold the breath and transfer the whole weight and our attention onto the other foot. Now exhale, hold the breath again whilst shifting our weight back to the front foot, inhale there, and repeat the exercise again. The exercise needs to be done for at least 10 minutes to be able to feel its beneficial effects.

Practices
This is one of the many practices that Bob Moore gave us. Practices can be used indefinitely, until the end of our lives and will continue to be effective.

Practice of observation or hara practice
The aim is to observe activity, especially emotional activity, and to achieve control through awareness. Such a control is different from suppression.

a) Bring light to the Individuality point. Move the light with your awareness down through the Crown chakra (do not stop there) to the Center of the Head. From there you move the light through the Pineal position on the forehead (third eye) out into the aura. Do not move too far out. Come back the same way to the Center of the Head. From there you continue with the light down to the Hara chakra, to the Perineum point between the legs (for men)/G-spot for the women and down to a point either between or underneath your feet. There you visualize the light as a ball full of light which you release before you continue. This whole movement should be done only once. 5-7 minutes.

b) All breathing only through the nose.

aa) Breathe in from an area around your head and move your awareness to the Hara, where after you let your awareness stay in the Hara during the next 5-6 breaths, in which you have to keep the following rhythm: inhale (count 4), pause (count 12), exhale (count 8). After exhaling there is no pause, even if it seems to feel natural. Do not produce stress. The above length of counting is just an example: the pause should be longest and the exhale the second longest. Inhale: pause: exhale should have a ratio of about 1:3:2.

bb) Let go of your Hara awareness during a 'Release breath': after 5 - 6 breaths in the way described above and after an exhale, breathe in and out suddenly and deeply through the mouth and nose at once. This is a quick movement. Do not be concerned about filling the lungs completely as it works mainly to clear energy built up on the etheric level. Repeat aa) and bb) all in all 5-10 minutes, stop with a Release breath. This part 'b' is a valuable exercise in itself, but then you do not move down with your awareness to the Hara.

c) Contact the light-ball at your feet again and let it move upwards as light through the Perineum point/G-spot to the Hara, where you let go of the contact.
2-3 minutes.

d) Visualize a calm lake with no surroundings and moonlight in it. You stand on the shore and look. It has to be the same lake, the same moonlight and you are standing in the same position each time you do this practice. Be aware of disturbances which may occur but return to the first clear picture*.
10 -15 minutes.

e)   Return to the light in the Hara chakra and move back and up with it the same way you came down with it under 'a' (Hara—Center of the Head—Pineal out and in—Center of the Head—Crown—Individuality point). Like on the way down, just do it once. 2-3 minutes.

The whole practice lasts 25 - 40 minutes.

'When there are no interferences in that picture any more you can use new pictures in part 'd' in the following order:

- Same lake but with moving clouds with moonlight in between
- Standing on a beach, looking at the sea with moonlight, gentle waves
- Same position on the beach but with a storm
- Looking at a mountain, sunrise over the mountain
- Same position, only with sunset

(from the book 'Conversations with Bob Moore')

Meditations

We can describe meditation as having four levels:

- **Concentration** – or how to control our busy mind or inner radio
- **Meditation** – or how to enter one experience and analyse it later
- **Contemplation** – or how to leave the physical level in order to get nearer to the essence or soul level
- **Illumination** and **silence**

How can we stop the inner radio from disturbing our meditation and observation? Bob called it the busy mind as opposed to the active mind. As this busy mind has disturbed observing minds for millennia, any culture, which practices introspective observation, has developed techniques to do so. The following are effective basic meditation techniques:

Observing one's breath

Find a quiet place and take 10 - 20 minutes.

If you have not done this before, five minutes is sufficient at the beginning. You can then augment the length of time as you feel. During the practise time sit with your spine straight without moving and place your palms on your thighs. Begin to watch your breath, allowing your breathing to become slower and deeper without forcing. This build up may take a while. Be aware of the belly extending out at each inhalation, this helps the diaphragm to move downwards and not block.

Observation of the body

After a period of deep, slow breathing we can direct our awareness to different parts of the body, in no particular order: left foot, belly, right foot, a knee, a hand, the shoulders, a thigh, a calf, neck and maybe again to one foot etc. Each time your mind starts to wander and the busy mind begins to takes over, move to another place on the body. This is a wonderful exercise for stilling the mind and for building up a better connection to the body.

Observation of an object
Focus on an object or a plant in front of you and bring your awareness back to it each time your mind becomes dispersed.

If your mind wanders do not to fight your thoughts, but gently take control of your awareness, so that you come back to the observation that you have set out to do. The positions of your hands are important. When sitting on a chair you can hold the palms of your hands either upwards or downwards, resting on your legs, Hands turned downwards will favour a better centring, upturned hands will bring more of an opening outwards.

Bob: "(In progressing) …we reach states of consciousness that allow us to blend different levels of our thoughts and our consciousness. That can take you beyond analysing and indeed can move you into another structure that takes you beyond the experiences. Many experiences are related to activity that is taking place between the etheric and the physical which involve emotional conditions. So it's possible to move beyond that.

So you come to the third stage in the progressive aspect of meditation and that is contemplation. Contemplation is what you can use to draw you beyond the influence of the activity of the physical body. So it gives you a means to reach a deeper aspect of yourself which some will call the soul level. Some, like myself, prefer to call it the essence. We have been using the movement of the spine to take us above the head.

In the progress in working with the front, back and centre of the spine it becomes possible to reach above the head. In reaching above the head then you come into a more true state of contemplation or a depth contact with yourself.

Then we come to the fourth stage which it seems to me has been very misunderstood, the state of enlightenment. That is open for everyone. It's not just for a selected few. If you are prepared to work with yourself, if you are prepared to really take on the control of yourself, you can reach enlightenment. That process of moving through these stages can bring you into stillness. That stillness is again something that one cannot describe. There are no words I could use to describe it. It's just that you are part of everything. This is what the reality of development is. "

For meditation to stay efficient and to avoid simply moving in unproductive circles, it needs to be progressive. That is why, we need either a meditation teacher who can follow our process closely or, if we meditate most of the time alone at home, we need to frequently change the structures of meditation, for instance every three months or, with some experience, every year.

Nobody has yet ever lived
Who would have surrendered themselves to the Divine
To the extent of not realising
That they could surrender even more.

Master Eckhardt

The Treatments

Who are actually we healing?

The words 'heal', 'healing' 'whole' and 'holy' are related. Spiritual healing endeavours to re-establish the 'holy whole', the original unity, the individuality = the indivisible duality. The spiritual or universal qualities of the chakras are showing us the way:

- acceptation of the bases of our life (root)
- peace of body and peace of mind (hara)
- love and understanding (solar plexus)
- compassion and joy (heart)
- expression (thyroid)

These are the emanations of the nature of the spirit, that is purity, light, vastness, with no beginning or end, and in perpetual creativity (construction-destruction-transformation).

Who are we trying to heal? Medical doctors and practitioners of all kinds of alternative forms of medicine are the specialists when it comes to alleviate physical ailments. They are often not trained to understand the deep causes and the meaning of illnesses. Most of the time they are specialised in one discipline and thus do not have a global understanding of the human being and all its systems. Patients ask them for an efficient and rapid relief of symptoms, and if possible without having to make any effort themselves. If we ask them to treat only the apparent malfunctioning part, in some way we are pushing them into a corner. They do what we are asking them to do. The spiritual healer does not try to do their job. Although it is often an illness that brings us to look for a spiritual, or a deeper healing, the main aim of spiritual healing is to lead the patient back to a state of peace. When a person finds peace within themselves and with the Divine, the body and the illness become somehow secondary. The primary aim is to guide a person into a transformation process and if physical problems can be healed at the same time, all the better. This does not mean neglecting the body or the physical pain but there may for example be karmic reasons, that make it is not possible to save or completely relieve the physical for the time being. The progression of the soul seems always to have priority.

In the film 'Healing', about the work of medium Joao de Deo, Dr. Henri Tjiong puts it this way:

"You must go back into your personal history, to all those times, when you became distant from the source or God, call it what you want. (These times) ….. cost you otherwise the connection to the source of all energy and all of Creation. That is ultimately where all illness comes from."

Harry Edwards in his book 'The Healing Intelligence' (p. 137): "There is a much wider purpose in spiritual healing than the mastering of physical and mental stresses." "The divine plan for all souls is that of spiritual progression." (p. 138): "As healing demonstrates the presence of spirit intelligences, so it establishes the fact of a spirit realm, to which, in the fullness of time, we are all heir to. To prove this, is the basic purpose behind spirit healing, to give mankind spiritual leadership in this age."

"After our physical death, our spiritual bodies continue to live in the world of spirits, capable to acquire wisdom, keeping our individual specificities and personalities as well as the potential of spiritual progression."

In his healing work Harry Edwards co-operated with numerous non-physical entities who had been medical specialists. The gifted medium Joao de Deo in Brazil is also working with non-physical entities under the guidance of Ignatius de Loyola.

Looking for the origins of physical and mental disorders
It is helpful to remember that our illnesses and disharmonies can stem from different sources:

- karmic
- emotional (including manipulations from the outside, trans-generational)
- hereditary, from birth
- pollution through substances and environment
- being exposed to excessive weather conditions (wind, cold, sun, heat, dryness)
- global movements (of fear e.g.)
- influences from the planets

I put the 'karmic' causes first because these can sometimes be linked to hereditary and emotional problems. Healing operates within the frame of the individual's deeper purpose and can only happen when the person is ready for it. Harry Edwards (p. 139): "Thus, before a spirit intelligence is able to heal the human mind and body an advanced process of learning has been necessary."

A hands-on healing treatment often starts on an etheric level, where disharmonies can be detected before becoming physical. Often we can detect an accumulation of energy on an etheric level, connected to a physical problem, that is already present or perhaps building up. We can then follow that energy which often leads us into the emotional field and often links up with the mental and possibly the causal aura.

This first check up on an energy level can often be done quite easily. In spiritual healing our focus is thus on looking beyond the etheric level as we are endeavouring to go back to the cause of the problem.

The etheric level stores all the memories connected to our sense perceptions (images, sounds, smells, touch, taste), whereas the emotional field (astral) stores the emotional charge connected to the event that we contact on the etheric level. Each event, each trauma will be stored at a specific place in the etheric. We can get a sense of how this comes about by studying the symbolism or deeper understanding of body parts. Other books have been written on this subject. The Chinese acupuncture meridian system can also give us some worthwhile hints as to these links. Bob gave us the following links :

> Thighs – shoulders – neck
> Chest/air area – genital area - feet
> Fire area/solar plexus – thighs – upper part of head
> Water area /Hara – knees – neck
> Calves – adrenals
> Shoulders – ankles – bottom of back

The example of the knees is very interesting: Knees on the physical level as on the emotional level are shock absorbers. The memory of shocks is therefore, partially stored there and this happens in time layers like the skins of an onion, the earliest event being stored next to the physical knee.

The mental field stores the thought patterns linked to that same event and the causal aura stores possible karmic or deeper causes from this life time. The reading of the aura and the interpretation is another step. Often in the talking part of a healing process, the healer is guided by intuition to address non-moving or stuck areas of the patient's mental aura, with the aim of bringing movement and growth, to allow the person to open towards their qualities. It can take time for the patient to integrate new understandings and then gradually change thought patterns. The interpretation of dreams can play a helpful part in the growth process.

Universal laws

Love, truth, attraction, cause and effect

The use and misuse of the word 'love' has often emptied it of its deeper content. It is necessary to reconnect to its deeper and universal meaning. Love, an eternal quality of the universe contains a deeply moving softness, a limitless patience, a well meaning attention, a wealth of wisdom and synthesis, and an unshakeable trust as well as maybe first of all its limitless strength.

I am constantly astonished by the deeper meaning of events, of things happening as if 'by chance' and the humour of the universe. A number of personal experiences have convinced me of the law of attraction, which brings exactly what we need on all levels and all times. This law will challenge our habits of escaping our personal responsibility by blaming others for things that happen in our own lives. These universal laws all seem to be linked. Attracting what we need is often linked to karmic or more recent events and this again seems to fit into the law of truth and love that are claiming their due.

The law of cause and effect brings us to pay back, sooner or later, whatever debt we have towards the laws of love and truth. Healing is thus linked to an inner maturation, a deepening insight into what compassion is. I believe that there can be lives, in a chain of incarnations, that are dedicated to atonement. Then there seem to be other lives where we rest and others where we are experimenting and testing the functioning of these laws and the power of our free will, even against all reason. The aim seems most likely to be that of strengthening our faith and wisdom to adhere to these laws whilst at the same time learning to handle our free will. I believe that our attitudes are tested, sometimes under very extreme conditions, in order to give us a learning opportunity to come out the other end somewhat wiser... sooner or later.

We may experience some difficulty – individually and collectively – of completely trusting the spiritual dimension and this might stem from difficult past experiences where we lost faith in God : "How can God, if he really exists, allow this to happen?" In a deep transformation process that is leading to our qualities and to higher consciousness, we may go through a time of releasing karmic memories linked to events where we lost faith. We can think of illnesses, accidents, natural catastrophes, torture, victims of terrorism, etc. How long would our faith withhold in such challenging situations? How long would we hold onto our faith and keep trusting?

The healing experience: seen from the healer's point of view.
Every healing session is first of all a sort of meditation, a practice in centring, observation and receptivity. Spiritual Healing needs us to be open to be guided by our feelings, our intuitions and perhaps to co-operate with evolved non-physical beings. After an introductory talk and beginning the healing part of the session we may simply need to wait and allow our intuition to guide our next steps. This can be a challenge because we find ourselves without known reference points. Our fears and insecurities may show up at this point. It is necessary to know how to still the busy mind and to be empty of ambition. We would also have to find the right

physical posture, in order to feel comfortable and not to block our own energy. We need to watch that we keep our wrists or fingers flexible and our shoulders loose; the arm streams move through them.

A type of centring exercise, in what ever form, is necessary before a healing treatment. It allows us to make contact with the three polarities: earth, heaven (light and higher consciousness) and heart energy.

Centring exercise

1. Contact a rhombus shaped area, the corners of which are the solar plexus, spleen point, liver point and navel. Breathe slow and deep into this zone and get a good feeling contact with it.
2. Contact the focus position above the head (see drawing p. 38)
3. Ask for guidance from a source of higher consciousness.
4. Place your attention into your feet and legs, feel the toes move and develop a good contact with every part of your legs and feet, until you feel well anchored.
5. Place your attention in the heart chakra and let a feeling of softness spread out from there.

Once we are well centred in those three dimensions it becomes easier to let ourselves be guided by our finer perceptions, so that we can be drawn to blockages or places on or around the body where we feel we can start the healing.

I suggest **starting** a healing with a period of talking so that the person can relax and open up. In this phase the two auras can blend, including the spiritual aura. After this, I would recommend that you place your hands on the person's shoulders, or if you feel that the person needs grounding, on the feet. You would also finish a session with a physical contact. The physical contact in the beginning helps both the healer's and the patient's energies to blend and allows the healer to get a feeling connection as to where to start.

We can **scan the energy fields** using different methods of perception (see p. 28). Using only one hand to do scanning does not set any healing treatment in motion. As soon as we use both hands, a circulation, including our arms and heart chakra starts to operate.

The healing can be focussing on any of the layers of the aura. While the work on the etheric alone may aim at momentarily releasing pain by dissipating an accumulation of energy, there is also another way of working on the etheric that includes other levels of consciousness. We mentioned a treatment that includes the reflector point and combines it with the pubic bone points. This work uses points on the etheric but by including the reflector point is bringing higher consciousness energy into the treatment.

Intuition is the most appropriate 'tool' to use in healing work as it is our intuition that leads our attention to certain areas, as for example, when we systematically scan the body with our felt sight or with our hands. We can for example get the impression of having to focus our treatment on the person's grounding/earth contact, on the legs and the corresponding energy points and streams. It is important to be patient and work slowly because the exchange of energy between just two points or between the left and the right side may require several minutes. We cannot dictate the rhythm of this work but have to be open for changes and impressions. With people who have a strong mental energy – this is often the case with men – longer work on the legs, feet and the hara is advisable. After a session it is always advisable to take time to reflect on what has happened in order to recall what the right brain may have registered but has not yet released into consciousness.

Bob: "The essential is that the person who receives healing contributes as well, without that it becomes an act of will force, which, in my opinion, is not spiritual healing, but the use of an activity of the etheric field."

To finish a treatment: An etheric massage which brings any freed energy back into the overall etheric circulation is an excellent way to end a treatment. We can move in the etheric with both hands up the left side on the front and down the left side on the back. Then move up at the back and down the front of the right side of the body. Repeat the movement on each side several times. (see p. 81)

The observation of the results of a healing treatment depends upon our perception and patience. We rarely have a complete overview of a person's development process. Sometimes we can have a feeling or notice an almost imperceptible change. Often we have to wait until the person can recognise their own changes, and they may or may not tell us.

The healing session seen from the patient's point of view: the time factor

Working with the hands in the etheric can sometimes have an immediate effect, as for example in relieving pain. This is not always the case with the work on the astral, mental, causal or spiritual energy field. The perceived effects depend largely on

Daniel Perret – The Science of Spiritual Healing

the sensitivity of the patient, and in these areas of the energy field the healing may work on the freeing of emotional and mental structures. When working on the mental aura a feeling of expansion around the head or chest area, can sometimes though be immediately felt. In the mental aura we tend to be working on stagnant thought patterns and limiting beliefs that underlie thinking (bad habits, guilt, lack of self-worth, inferiority etc). The effects can last up to 36 hrs after a treatment.

A healing session can include a therapeutic talk, prayer, meditation and energy awareness exercises. After a healing session a person can contact a freer, more open way of thinking and is likely to have new or more intuitive thoughts. Pain may get temporarily worse and emotions can be released both during and after a healing session. We can also witness a deep emotional clearance. There may be helpful dreams during the nights following the session. The results of a healing session may not be felt right away, but in the days and weeks following the treatment the patient may suddenly gain new insight into a previously stuck situation. It may be that he suddenly becomes aware of having another perception of himself, feeling lighter, less negative, and feels freedom from certain emotional patterns or notices a change in a habitual way of reacting. It is not always easy to pinpoint the effects of a single healing treatment, but when working over several months or longer with the same person, it is moving to see the subtle and deep changes that can come about on every level.

Healing through sound
In my book 'Sound healing and the five elements' I have underlined the importance of linking consciousness to the use of sound. One of the ways that I like to work with sound is that use the tone quality of a musical instrument or of specific

sounds to guide my consciousness towards zones in the energy field where there is a blockage or a blind spot.

The metaphor of the five elements *earth, water, fire, air* and *space* allows us to discern the quality of a sound and to predict its impact. We can then get in contact more easily with the blind spots or blockage zones and use our consciousness to bring the trapped energy back into circulation. The psycho-energetic exercises that we learned from Bob Moore make this work with sounds even more efficient. The sounds themselves can have an impact that can last several days. I always encourage the patient to link sound work to consciousness (energy awareness exercises). We can use sound and music to trigger emotions, but my focus is rather on the lasting and beneficial effects of sound and therefore a conscious co-operation from the patient is necessary.

Obviously music can be used successfully for relaxation, for opening up our hearts and right brain, for inspiration and contact with higher consciousness. It can also be used in active music therapy which consists of a dialogue with an individual or a group of patients, using simple musical instruments in order to access different aspects of the energy system through the use of the five elements (for this aspect of music therapy see my book 'Roots of Musicality'). Music therapy can for example be help someone contact their emotions, especially if they have repressed them and have a little contact with their body. In sound healing our aim is different aim, we use the direct impact of sound without any musical dialogue.

During healing sessions we do not recommended using music. Music tends to keep people on a certain emotional level and may not allow an opening to take place. Bob: "Silence is the inner part of sound. All sound moves in a spiral and the inner core of that spiral is silence and that is what you are contacting with your qualities in healing, So silence is one of the most important facets in healing."

Healing through colour

Bob taught us how to use eight colours with the help of a light source to produce a beneficial effect in the aura. We place Lee filters (stage lighting filters) under a transparent quartz crystal that is standing on top of a lamp so that the colour of the filter is diffused. We can place the colour lamp in a room and it will have a beneficial effect on the atmosphere. We can also use the colours in meditative processes and transfer the feeling of the colour with our awareness towards certain zones of our energy fields. The use of sound should precede the use of colours if both are used during a treatment, as sound precedes colour in general in all creation. Colour healing is a vast subject, which we will not go into in this book.

Hands-on healing

This way of healing uses the energy that is transmitted through the healer's hands and particularly the secondary chakras in the hands. An energy circulation is created between the two hands, the heart, the pineal and thyroid chakras and the aura of the patient. Obviously the energy field of the healer and much wider energy fields take part in this as well. Her hands (and eyes) help to direct the energy with great precision. The healer can also work at a distance from the body in the astral, mental or spiritual aura. Her hands guide her as if they were sense organs, helping her to feel different types of energy and information. The hands also provide an entry point into deeper aspects of intuition and finer perception. Experience, faith, a link with non-physical beings or other dimensions and the understanding of the energy structures around a person are the bases of this work. I have seen people working exclusively in the etheric near to the physical body, simply because they did not understand anything about the other layers of the aura. In my experience, in healing work as with spontaneous artistic expression we allow energy to flow through us and don't exactly know where it is coming from. We can though learn to distinguish between emotional and spiritual energy.

Bob: "If you have a really good contact with your qualities then you are producing a quicker movement of energy, a quicker vibration of energy in the other person's aura. You are directing that either with your eyes or with your hands. The other person's response to that is their healing process and in their response they are automatically drawing to what you have to give and of course, if you are giving it from a higher aspect of yourself that is the attraction point."

"When you use two hands you are always in a healing process. You may be sensing but at the same time you are healing or you are creating a healing effect. If you are just using one hand then the healing effect is much less and the reason for that is because you haven't built up a continuity in yourself between your thoughts and the rhythm of movement. The reality of any process of healing is what contact you have achieved with your own qualities and that essentially must link to your own heart connection. ... When you move (the) energy (of the blockage) outward in a process of healing you are drawing on your own qualities."

In the film 'Healing' Dorothy W. Cooke: "This all has to do with energy. All we are doing here is energy work, light work. It has all to do with energy. Because that is what we are: energy."

Using one's fingers

When working on specific energy points we can use the fingertips of the major (+) and ring fingers (-), either together or the positive finger on one point and the negative finger on the other. Wait until the energy flow is established between the fingers, and until the flow clearly diminishes. This can take several minutes.

Protection

Bob: "You can't protect yourself by closing in, then you are more vulnerable, you can only protect yourself by moving outward and in this way again you are uplifted." It is fear that makes us close off and become vulnerable. The best protection is love, understanding and being open. In order to achieve this you need, after a treatment or teaching, to go over the exchanges (words, feelings and other observations of the right brain – thus often subconscious) you have had with people, either after each session or at the end of the day. This allows you to open up to the subconscious effects. It is not unusual, during or after a treatment, to register pain in our physical body that comes from the other person. If this is happening it is advisable to ask whoever we feel is assisting us in our work (non-physical guide) to help us to register the information intuitively so that it does not penetrate us physically. Equally we can have words or subtle observations that have not entered our consciousness completely, but that will continue to affect us if we do not become aware of them and deal with them. In order to stay compassionate we need to expand our consciousness, taking into consideration these effects.

The solar plexus chakra needs to have a good balance of drawing in and extension out of energy. The same for the spleen and liver secondary chakras, they need to have a good extension out of energy. Both these streams need to be balanced so that one is not stronger than the other.

Before a healing session it is advisable to make sure what contact the person has with their emotions, their qualities and how well they are expressing themselves.

Healing from the spiritual level
A considerable part of our energy resonates with the energy of the people present in a room, and even more so with the energy of the patient upon whom we direct all our attention. Our etheric, emotional, mental and spiritual fields participate in this movement. In order to be as conscious as possible of what is going on in the interaction between the energy fields it the necessity to know oneself.

In spiritual healing we call upon love, light or higher consciousness energy - the most penetrative and powerful energy. In order for these energies to work it is necessary to have established this higher consciousness contact with ourselves and also for the patient to place trust in us. It is only then that our energy fields can interact on a deeper level. When this blend happens little more than perhaps a prayer is needed. We are not alone when we work with healing and higher levels of consciousness and evolved beings may take over or contribute the main part at this point.

"It is the karmic issues that can prevent a further deepening of the individual's process, if they are not dealt with. It is sacredness that penetrates these layers of karmic structures.
It is love that heals and transforms them.
It is the light of conscience that alters the focus of the mind."

A.R. channelled by Eva Høffding

Daniel Perret – The Science of Spiritual Healing

Distant healing

Praying or sending distant healing to others with the help of evolved spirits is an important part of a spiritual healing process. I believe that non-physical beings and many dimensions of higher consciousness are involved in this. Many studies have documented the efficiency of distant healing and prayer. (see books like the ones of the English healer Harry Edwards). A person's free choice must as far as possible, be respected so it is always important that they have asked for or agree to receive healing. It is possible to make exceptions if special circumstances (comas, no access) make it impossible to ask directly. It is different for prayer, which is often used without the explicit consent of the receiver. We should also be careful with prayer not to invade someone with good intentions or our own emotional motives.

The impact of distant healing will be enhanced if the receiver tunes in at the same time as the distant healing is happening. Distant healing can be done alone or with a group of people in the same room or in different locations, using the same time of day and length of time (15 minutes.) The following or similar procedures are often used:

Distant healing:

- centre yourself in you heart
- contact your ID-point
- come back to your heart
- expand the energy outwards in front of you
- while contacting gold briefly and
- ask for help whoever you feel like asking : the universe, the source, higher consciousness, a divine source
- you can then refer to a list of names that you want to include in this distant healing session

Can we damage someone during a healing treatment?

We will not damage someone if we have the right motivation – that is the wish to bring support, love and compassion to others.

When, in our daily lives, we abide by the universal laws of love and truth, progressively centre ourselves in our heart contact, and have good grounding that allows us to deepen our contact to our subconscious and the three lower chakras this brings balance and harmony to our work with others. You will rarely find warnings or forbidden paths in this book simply because a pure motivation is all that is needed.

If at some point during a healing session the energy does not seem ready, our intuition can for example, indicate not to use healing that day and we must respect this. A correct motivation safeguards us against discarding such precious information. As higher levels of consciousness guide us, we are only one part of a healing session. It helps to remember 'Thy will be done' – not ours. Joy in what we are doing will indicate that we are working with the right motivation.

Transition

It is the mind that creates separation and holds you back
Into fear and what you call depression.
See it from the other side, your soul is longing for you,
Longing to welcome you home and nourish you in softness.
Change your perspective, let go of these shackles,
Open your heart to yourself in all your beauty.
Cease all pushing and hardness, you will succeed
when you accept that as you are, you are enough,
You have all you need within.

Marie Perret 1998

The Field

Rupert Sheldrake and his well known theory of morphogenetic fields explained how collective knowledge could be transmitted through the etheric of the earth, the akasha records, to other beings. This brief chapter will endeavour to place the science of spiritual healing in a context and give give a brief overview of the following themes: fields of research, fields of experience, mental fields, spiritual and universal fields of wisdom that relate to the science of spiritual healing.

I have been inspired in my own research by the following authors like Jakob Bösch and healers like the American Edgar Cacey, the Englishman Harry Edwards, the German Bruno Gröning, the Brazilian John of God, the Philippine Alex Orbito, the French Philippe de Lyon but also evolved spirit beings like Ignacio de Loyola. I feel that the needs of the time we live in is bringing about an increased co-operation between physical and non-physical beings.

Cooperating with evolved non-physical beings

Spirit guides (saints and other evolved beings), angels (of inspiration, guardian angels, body elementals), archetypal forces (Marie, Christ, God, Holy Spirit and the corresponding non-Christian expressions), other evolved non-physical beings

Today the spiritual realms seem to be interested in co-operating with healers or study groups that consciously link healing with personal development, as for example the use of exercises taught by Bob Moore. I have been surprised to realise that these invisible worlds seem to need our co-operation as much as we need theirs. Everything seems to be connected, even between these very different levels. Faith healing is an essential part of Christian beliefs (as it is with shamanism), much more so than for instance within Buddhism.

I believe that, just as there are energy fields that is non-visible aspects of ourselves, there exist a multitude of levels of consciousness or levels of existence inhabited by beings with different tasks. Each one co-operates with others and seems to be directed by beings that are more evolved.

This is the case with **nature spirits** or nature intelligences that perform multiple and complex tasks that are mostly unknown to us. We have to ask ourselves how complex biological systems function and keep such delicate balances, if we wish to grasp the field of action and important role of nature spirits. Without specialised intelligences no plant, no tree, no river, no natural thing would function properly. We know how difficult it is to maintain the balance of an outdoor swimming pool's water. This is a very simple system as there is no life in an artificial swimming pool, no plant life, newts or fishes, no micro-organisms.

The excellent series published by the 'Flensburger Hefte' have taught me a lot about the work of nature intelligences. Marko Pogacnik has given an excellent introduction into the work of higher nature beings that are in charge of valleys, rivers, a whole landscape or a forest. If, all by ourselves, we had to look after the delicate balance of a natural pond, a source or underground water reserves, we would not know where to start. We see how difficult this is when we try to restore natural environments that have been polluted.

I believe that we are also assisted by a number of invisible beings during our lives, from conception, pregnancy, birth, the difficult moments of life until death and beyond. We have until now called them 'angels' or 'guardian angels'. Reality seems more complex. It would seem to me (I'm using the conditional form, as I am basing what I write here on other people's experiences, on books as well as my own limited experience) that we each have a **body elemental** who looks after our body and its different systems. He is meant to work without us knowing as his task is thus not interrupted by our emotions and will. He gets his instructions from more evolved beings.

Then we all have, I'm convinced, an **evolved non-physical being** or one or more spirit guides that are close to this notion of guardian angel but are not part of the angelic world. They are non-physical beings (former doctors, saints or highly developed women or men) who have previously lived on earth, and who continue their selfless work from the spirit world. Not being physical makes their work much easier, even if they no longer have access to our spectrum of experiences (emotions, senses, able to move things physically etc.). Depending upon our needs the same guide or evolved being would be accompanying us through several life times. They are accessible to us through our feelings and intuitions, sometimes in dreams, and certainly through sincere mediums. In my experience Bob Moore continues to work with healing even after his death.

I like this story where a human being asks his guardian angel: "I can see two pairs of footprints in the snow behind me, even if I don't see you. But in my difficult moments I can see only one pair. Why is it that precisely when I need you most you leave me alone?" "The reason why you only see one pair of footprints in those difficult moments is because I am carrying you in my arms."

I believe and experience, mainly through my feelings, that beyond our personal guide we have access to other evolved non-physical beings. During a healing session or in a development group we can often be surrounded by those beings. They guide us, watch us or simply learn from us. No longer being physical themselves, they need us to do or understand certain things that they cannot do or perceive themselves.

Depending on our beliefs we give these beings different names. There are, what I would call, powerful **universal archetypes** such as the Mary energy which I have felt to be as vast as the universe or like the starry sky, full of love, softness and grace. Other cultures, other religions have given her different names. It would seem to me that what we call the **Christ energy** does not belong to one religion. I have felt that energy as luminous, joyous, filling my whole body down to the bottom of my torso, at the same time it is gentle and powerful. There is an archetypal energy that exists in all religions, that Christians call the **Holy Spirit** energy, which I have experienced this as being somehow horizontal. At times I perceive and feel it in all reflections of light: on a leaf, on water, on a cloud. I'm still exploring this. There are also hierarchies of **angelic beings**, probably linked to the whole creation process. I sometimes feel the presence of an 'angel of inspiration' when I compose.

If we are co-operating with non-physical beings during a healing session, the question arises as to what our role is. They are present and very active when we work with energy or teach a group, so to what extent do they need us? Can they not do their work without us, are we an interference? I believe when we invite them to participate and all people present in a group open themselves in trust that this allows them to come nearer and intervene. Our level of consciousness and openness towards the non-physical realms attracts them to us. In a way we create a channel, an access, a pathway and our energy field facilitates their work. It seems that they also need to use a part of our etheric (ectoplasm) for the healing work. All of this, let us remember, is linked to their total respect of our free will. The more we are working with our mental and spiritual aura and our level of consciousness rises, the more we will be able to co-operate with evolved beings and ultimately co-operate with the divine energy of love and light. As this happens it is likely that we will be using our hands much less to work with healing in someone's energy fields.

There are also the phenomena of **collective thought forms** linked to a place, consisting of a collective human creation on a mental level built up through the projections of the desires and emotional intensity of a great many people. These places (Lourdes, Majagori, Knock) can be very powerful energy centres and sometimes trigger miraculous healings or important changes in a person's beliefs and thought patterns. Patterns that were limiting the person can be dissolved and transformed through faith and visiting such places or participating in a mass event. These collective thought forms can contain different energies, from astral, emotional up to higher consciousness energy.

Where I come from
I deeply respect people's religious beliefs and feel akin to all religious people, be they Shamans, Animists, Buddhists, Taoists, Mohammedans or other. I cannot deny my Christian background, in the sense that I grew up with it and lived my

life influenced by it to a lesser or greater degree. However since my twenties I have been involved in a process of personal growth that has taken me into a connection with spirituality that lies beyond religious structures.

Although I have never doubted the existence of non-physical entities, it is only in recent years that I explore this theme more actively, endeavouring to reach beyond the beliefs I received as a child. I am carefully choosing the words I use in writing about non-physical beings, who are clearly beyond any division or sectarianism, so as not to exclude anyone, for instance, from another religion.

I am happy to see that an evolved non-physcal being like Ignatius of Loyola changed his vocabulary since the 16th century. Today he speaks about approaching the 'divine field' or the 'Christhood material', which is a terminology I feel I can identify with because it does not exclude anyone. All religious paths, Shamanistic and Animistic included, have almost the same 'archetypes' and evolved beings, which are similar to ours.

I aim to be discriminating and cautious in order to evaluate

- The quality of non-physical beings involved
- The terminology used, that reaches beyond any particular religion
- My cultural beliefs
- The usefulness for anyone who is open to these dimensions

The co-operation with non-physical dimensions happens because of our receptivity and through our invitation. As our free will is a condition that we must adhere to, it is important to be vigilant and to make sure that any being that we link to, physical or non-physical, operates according to these criteria:

> Respect of free choice, compassion, joy, humbleness and truth.

These are the same criteria that a healer or therapist has to observe. I am convinced that all terminology, all description of the qualities of beings and levels involved must reflect a truth that has existed before any religion or church and that would continue to exist long after.

In my teaching and healing work I ask non-physical beings to help me to be open and receptive to their guidance and to assist me. I can sometimes see them, and watch what they are doing and notice the quality of their presence, without necessarily understanding all I see.

Forms of spiritual healing

> Brief overview: folk healers, Philippino healers, Maître de Lyon, Edgar Cayce, Harry Edwards, folk healers, shamans, Bob Moore, Joao de Deo and his team of non-physical evolved beings

I want to give credit to the numerous healers, **ordinary people with special healing gifts** who often work anonymously and who come from an oral tradition. Their gifts have often been transmitted to them through a parent and this has sometimes been passed down through several generations in their family. Some have the gift of being able to take away warts or remove the fire when somebody has burnt themselves. The cleaning lady at the children's day clinic where I worked realised that she could even heal burns over the phone. Scientists have recently proved that oral traditions are far more accurate than written traditions. It is difficult to understand how enormous books of wisdom like the Indian Upanishads were for centuries, if not millennia, transmitted orally before being written down in the Middle-Ages. I am convinced that nothing got lost during this long period of oral transmission.

We started this book by stating that felt knowledge or wisdom, learned through one's own experience is completely different from information acquired from books. All the Shamanic traditions have been transmitted orally, including those in Europe, until the druids, wise women and men were persecuted and burnt. It is a mistake to think that human beings from other times or continents were and are uneducated primitives, of low of intelligence. All forms of Spiritual healing emerged from the immense intuitive wisdom of these folk traditions and their link to nature and to spiritual dimensions - that is from 'normal', humble people, with good common sense, their feet firmly on the ground and their hands on their hearts. What must they all think of us now that our way of living and exploiting the earth is breaking down because of our lack of basic natural intelligence, common sense and respect.

In Brazil there is an important healing centre: the Casa Dom Ignacio de Loyola where numerous non-physical entities perform operations through the medium Joao de Deo, or **John of God**. These evolved beings have, during their life on earth, been medical doctors and surgeons and continue to practise their art for the benefit of human beings. Hundreds of thousands of people have visited the Casa and received healing there. Documentary films show different operations, this is the part that is visible to the cameras. The camera shows Joao using rudimentary surgical instruments, sometimes even simple knives, when operating on eyeballs, cutting into the skin of the stomach area or when introducing a type of scissor into the nostrils. Joao is a complete trance medium – this means that entities incorporate into his physical body whilst he is unconscious. The healing work at the Casa is based on **faith healing**, which means that the healer and the patient believe in the limitless healing power of the Divine. At the Casa or similar places the healing work is based on faith, and does not involve psychotherapy or teaching personal development.

At the Casa they also perform **invisible operations**. These can affect the physical level as well as all other levels. On a physical level medical doctors have reported seeing stitches inside the body, whilst looking with an ultrasound scanner, when no trace of an incision could be found on the outside. These operations differ from pure spiritual healing by being more precisely located. Joao's nose operations seem to be about gaining access energetically, in some puzzling way, to the inside of the body. The explanation is missing, but as so often in this field, the results are convincing. See the excellent DVD on the work in the Casa Dom Ignacio 'Healing' by David Unterberg. www.healing-themovie.com

I have benefited from such invisible operations, under the guidance of Ignatius de Loyola, during retreats in Denmark. On one occasion I felt unusual rapid movements to and fro in front of my stomach area. Afterwards the entities informed me, when I asked them, that they had operated on all levels of my being, that would mean karmic, emotional, mental, etheric, physical levels. The dreams I had in the following nights certainly confirmed this. It is obvious to me that we have evolved beings that have an astonishing knowledge, compassion and intelligence that goes way beyond my understanding. At the same time they show us what is possible to reach.

In the film of 2010 'Healing' Dr. Henri Tjiong relates the story of a friend of his who was in hospital in Germany and who had asked for healing. He sent a photograph to the Casa and Dr. Tjiong asked the entities if he could have a surrogate operation done on him for his friend. They agreed. "The next day he had an ultrasound pictures taken und this showed indeed some inner stitches. Nothing could be seen from the outside. The Doctors gathered around his bed and asked him: 'Where did you get this operation done on you?' He said: 'What operation. I was all the time here.' 'No, you had an operation done on you. We can see this on the ultrasound pictures.' 'Ask the sisters. I was here in the hospital all the time.'

In the same film, Anjelika Kremer: "Most entities that work through the medium Joao had been former healers, medical doctors or priests. They are very familiar with emotional and physical diseases. Through his (Joao's) consciousness they transmit messages to you. They can scan you und make an x-ray picture of your insides. They know exactly what is happening to you. Before you can at all formulate your question, they already have the answer. They know what you have come with."

Healing through the combination of faith, meditation and development exercises
The difference between the Casa in Brazil and my approach is that I combine faith, meditation and the conscious work with Bob's exercises. My own direct perceptions of beings like Ignatius de Loyola were of a feeling kind. I can also sometimes sense the violet colour that surrounds him or feel his light touch on my shoulder. I would also perceive differences in the quality of the presence of the different entities present.

Whilst still alive, **Bob Moore** used to work with his hands and his awareness (that is his mental and spiritual field) on and above the physical body. His work as a healer went through a number of phases. In the 70's he often worked in the energy fields using his hands, sometimes together with his wife Anni. He would often work on a person three times in the same week. His skill in combining his intuitive awareness with talking allowed him to be highly effective just sitting opposite the person without using his hands. During the last ten years that he worked Bob probably did not use his hands anymore in healing and would only give individual sessions to pupils of his who were in a development process. He felt that it was vital for a person to contribute to their own healing process by working consciously on themselves.

See also the excellent documentaries on DVD's, in French though, of Yves Bilien or Bernard Bonnamour on Maître Philippe de Lyon.
http://www.filmsdocumentaires.com/7-spiritualite

The **Shamanic traditions** of natives in Africa, Siberia, South-America, North-America, also work with healing and also co-operate with non-physical beings. This can be nature spirits and also evolved non-physical beings.

The **Philippino healers**, like Alex Orbito, seem to work essentially on the etheric body. A characteristic of their way of working is that they insert their hands into the physical body of the person and pull objects or substances of apparently organic matter out from inside the body. They are essentially faith healers, working in a Christian context.

Internet, mass media and books have contributed to the diffusion of a collective knowledge about these different healing traditions. The evolution of our levels of consciousness contributes to the co-operation with the non-physical realms. The increasing vulnerability of human and natural systems today leads us towards this co-operation. Considerable opening and progress in the fields of research and experience in the domain of spiritual healing have been achieved in recent years.

Other forms of treatments

The following diagram is a brief comparison between different forms of treatment and is obviously simplified. The level of consciousness and personality of the healer determines the specific characteristics of any system.

Psychotherapy	Shamanism	Spiritual Healing	Acupuncture
Process takes place over several months or years	Process in its particular space and organisation (4 directions, heaven, earth, etc.)	Process takes place in the present but needs sometimes several sessions in same week	A series of sessions can be necessary
gradual steps	Sudden changes possible	Gradual or sudden changes	Often immediate effects on etheric and physical level
therapist guides the healing process	The shaman and the spirits take care of the healing	spirits and/or healer	Practitioner, ev. assisted by non-physical levels
Mobilises the inner resources of the patient	Resources exterior to the patient	Depending on the healer	The chi of the practitioner

Quite direct	Often complex preparations	Easy access, Depends on the healer	Easy access
training	Inherited or training	Gift or training	Training
Therapist is paid with money	The shaman gets presents	Depends on the tradition of the healer	Therapist is paid with money
Spoken	Ritualised language, chants, frame drum, shaker	Spoken language or non-spoken, hands-on healing	Depending on practitioner, usually little talking, using hands and needles
Mainly on mental and emotional level	On all levels	On all levels	Mainly on the etheric level
Individual or group session	Everybody is invited to assist	Individually or in group	individually or (in Chine often) in presence of other patients

Spontaneous artistic expression

Spontaneous and authentic feeling expression is the fourth tool I am working with, the other three being meditation, psycho-energetic exercises and the cooperation with non-physical beings. I attach much importance to spontaneous expression because of its link with the thyroid chakra, the chakra of expression, which forms a synthesis of the four lower chakras and is responsible for bringing that energy up to the pineal chakra. In order to function as freely and efficient as possible, the thyroid chakra needs a direct, authentic and spontaneous expression coming from within. In order to reach this it is essential not to censure our expression. All types of expression contribute to the balanced functioning of the thyroid chakra: words, actions, thoughts, dreams. It is necessary to find forms of expression that allow our deeper feelings and subtle perceptions to come forward. Any authentic expression, which links inner feelings and outer expression is essential to a process of transformation and liberation (see also my other books.)

Spontaneous painting and also expression through sound and improvised music that I teach are forms of expression that are very useful in this context. In so doing we aim to free ourselves from external authority or expectations from others. These forms of expression emphasise the process in the present and are to be totally free of ambition or focus on product.

Healing the Earth
We cannot heal ourselves without healing the planet.
We cannot heal the planet without healing ourselves.
All begins with the experience of harmony and peace in us.

Coming to the end of this book on the science of spiritual healing I would like to underline the importance of being aware that all life on this planet is sacred and utterly interdependent. Healing is part of the unique beauty of life. He underlines the importance of the work on ourselves, if we really want to be able to heal the earth.

No healer can copy another as each person has a unique energy and needs to discover how to use their individual qualities. I have placed much emphasis on the method and the process in this book, because the most important thing is to develop our own intuitive way of working. Energy structures can be useful starting points but they are not the beginning and end of everything. It is the continuous inner search for the spiritual and divine dimension and the development of compassion that guarantees that we progress and not remain in limitations. Until we really know and love ourselves, this journey will never come to an end.

Sometimes in our lives when we doubt, and do not to see any progress, then perhaps we could ask ourselves the question : 'In what state of spiritual and physical health would we be if we had not undertaken anything in terms of our spiritual development, therapy or healing ? Have we avoided serious illnesses or difficulties? Will we ever have an answer to this question?

Dordogne, May 2010

"When you ... are ill, than your soul is telling you to wake up. Life gives you gentle invitations to wake up, all along your life. When you are seriously ill it is like a cold shower poured all over you and you must wake up. This is difficult, but it is a great opportunity to find out who you really are."

Phoebe, a young Australian in the Film 'Healing'

Appendices

A) Left and right hemisphere of the brain

Left hemisphere of the brain	Right hemisphere of the brain
Corresponding to right side of body	Corresponding to left side of body
male principle	Female principle
expression, performance	Receptivity
intellect and linear analysis	Innovation, intuition, inspiration
cause and effect relationship	Search for sense
sequential treatment	Global treatment and view (atmosphere)
sense of quantity	sense of quality
material level	energy and spiritual level
grammar, vocabulary	poetic value of words and phrases
semantic	perception of shapes and forms
	visual-constructive tasks
	perception of own body, emotions and feelings
	awareness of self and of imagination
in healing	*in healing*
techniques, theory, lexical knowledge	following ones intuition

B) Definitions of mind and consciousness

There are different definitions of mind. The psycho-energetic views **mind** as a conglomerate of the upper astral where our feelings reside, the upper mental levels, the individual spiritual level where our innate qualities are found together with the spiritual layers beyond the individual. Tibetan Buddhism describes the nature of mind by distinguishing between *sem*, the intellect known also as our lower mental field and *rigpa* or the ultimate essence of mind which is the basis for any abiding comprehension. These teachings suggest that only the experience of pure mind allows us to know the nature of absolute reality. "It is simply your flawless, present awareness, cognizant and empty, naked and awake." (Sogyal, 1992). Buddhism is at the same time pragmatic and metaphysical in its approach to mind. "No words can describe it … it has never been born …it has no limits at all…" (Dudjom Rinpoche in Sogyal 1992).

These definitions are clear, simple and at the same time open, thus taking into consideration the fact that we actually know very little when it comes to consciousness and the mind and that words are a very restrictive and inadequate means to express what we do know.

In Indian philosophy, essentially still present and alive in the millenary traditions of yoga and Hinduism, the definitions of consciousness and mind are very similar to the definitions in Buddhism. Buddhism incorporates huge chunks of Hinduism as well as rejecting certain central aspects of Hinduism such as the caste system. Buddhism was of course formed in the midst of Hindu culture. The reason why Buddhism, Hinduism and Chinese Taoism are such rich sources of understanding when it comes to the nature of mind, as well as for all that is beyond the physical and the visible, comes from the fact that the founders and practitioners of these traditions have been studying the subject for millennia and have no trouble accepting the existence of invisible energy. The encyclopedic dictionary of Yoga by Georg Feuerstein (1990) for instance offers us a rigorous and clear approach to the subject based fundamentally on pragmatic self observation. In the Indian tradition, the lower mental or intellect is called *manas*. In the yogic tradition *manas* is considered as a sense because of its close resemblance to the processes of the five senses. Accordingly, its operational ways are anchored in desire, willfulness, doubt, irresolution, shame, knowledge (I guess they mean 'received knowledge or opinion' here as opposed to personal knowledge), fear, belief, lack of belief and discipline. This makes of *manas* a suspect and unreliable tool.

The neuroscientist Antonio Damasio in his book "The Feeling of What Happens" (Damasio, 1999) ventured into a deep research of **consciousness** and its mechanisms. In it he reminds us of the necessity to make a distinction between 'mind', 'consciousness', 'moral conscience', 'soul' and 'spiritual'. He believes that the consciousness of a person can be described as 'the real sense that a person has got of herself and her surroundings'. He suggests considering consciousness as being a part of mind, the conscious part. "There can be mind without consciousness, as can be observed with patients that have got only one without the other." After this observation he focuses on what consciousness is and how it manifests on a brain level, warning us at the same time that "Understanding consciousness says nothing or very little about the origin of the Universe, the meaning of life nor of their probable destinies." Consciousness, according to Damasio, is at the beginning a feeling of what happens when we see, hear and touch. He underlines thus how much consciousness is anchored in our bodies and our physical sensations.

Bina John emphasises the point that to understand the link between music and mind, we need to include emotions in the definition of consciousness, the neurological as well as the spiritual aspects of the experience (John, 2003). She is convinced that musical education must start from a feeling basis including experiences of a spiritual kind, those filled with meaning, so as to motivate young children to engage with music. Stanley Greenspan (1997) agrees that our emotional development is essential for any further form of development.

The definition of consciousness does not necessarily include any moral conscience (since moral conscience is only partially conscious), but does embrace a number of different levels of consciousness as well as the awareness of oneself. Consciousness is the **conscious part of mind** capable of observing phenomena that take place on different levels whether physical, emotional, mental or energetic and which relates them to the observing self. Consciousness has the faculty to be aware of itself, to associate with ourselves the observations we make about our body and our whole psycho-energetic system, and it can discern the differences in phenomena that do not concern us.

Again the explanation in Buddhist and Yogic traditions help to clarify the issue (Feuerstein, 1990). They draw our attention to the numerous traps and illusions concerning our knowledge of the human mind. To find access to really liberated states of consciousness they suggest learning to stabilise five functions of mind and only then learning to detach oneself from them. These are exact perception of the material world, intellectual knowledge, conceptualisation or intellectually chewing over things, lethargy, laziness and sleepiness of mind and finally lexical memory. In this book the word 'spiritual' means the source of mind reaching beyond the human intellectual mind. In India the Hindu tradition calls it *atman*.

It is said in the Talmud that when Adam and Eve were chased from paradise, God saw that a great loneliness had come over them. He decided then, out of compassion, to give them the gift of tears.

And a bit further on: Even when the gates of heaven seem to stay closed to our prayers, they always remain open to our tears.

Bibliography

Bailey, A., her works, Editions Lucis Trust
Bösch, Jakob, , Spiritual Healing and Medical Science',
ISBN 978-3-03800-281-9
Flensburger Hefte, interviews with nature spirits in german,
www.flensburgerhefte.de
Cayce, E., his works, www.arecatalog.com
Dalaï Lama, ,The Universe in a single atom', Barnes & Noble
Edwards, H., ,The Healing Intelligence', Healer Publishing Co., 1965
Gamborg, H. ,Das Wesentliche ist unsichtbar', Rororo, Opus Verlag
Gilkeson, J. 'Energy Healing', Marlow & Co., New York, 2000
Gilkeson, J. 'A Pilgrim in Your Body', Universe Inc., New York, 2009
Helliwell, T. 'A summer with the Leprachauns', Blue Dolphin Pub. 1997
Odoul, M., 'Dis-moi où tu as mal, je te dirais pourquoi.', A.Michel, 2002
Moore, R.S., Mauthner A. + A. 'Conversations with Bob Moore, 1992
Perret, D. 'Music–The feeling Way', 1997, free download on our website
Perret, D. 'Roots of Musicality', Jessica Kingsley Publishers, 2004
Perret, D. 'Sound healing with the five elements', Binkey Kok, 2007
Perret, D. 'The concrete experience of spirituality', manuscript 2010
Perret, M. 'Spontane Kreativität', Drachenverlag, Klein Jasedow, 2008
Pogacnik, M. 'Nature Spirits and Elemental Beings', Findhorn Press, 1996
Pogacnik, M. 'Healing the Heart of the Earth', Findhorn Press, 1998
Schore, A. 'Affect Regulation and the Repair of the Self'', W.W.
Norton & Co, 2003
Van Kampenhout, D. ,Images of the Soul', Carl-Auer-Systeme Verlag
Auteur inconnu, 'Cloud of Unknowing', Hodder & Stoughton
Christian Classics

Daniel Perret – The Science of Spiritual Healing

Biography

Daniel Perret was born in Zurich in 1950. He studied economics at the University of Zurich and then worked for 15 years as a socio-cultural community worker. In 1990 he moved to Dordogne, South-West of France, with his wife Marie Perret, an art-therapist, and their son. He studied Spiritual Healing with Bob Moore in Denmark from 1979 to 1999 together with his wife. Since1981 he has been teaching courses in music therapy and spiritual healing in different European countries, mainly France, Switzerland and Ireland. From 1996 until 2010 he worked as a music therapist in at Brive hospital with children with developmental disorders. As a musician and composer he has recorded over thirty albums. He is the author of several books on music and healing.

Daniel Perret – The Science of Spiritual Healing

Centre du Vallon (Dordogne)
Berboules
F - 24290 Sergeac
www.vallonperret.com

Daniel Perret – The Science of Spiritual Healing